JACQUES ELLUL

JACQUES ELLUL

Essential Spiritual Writings

Selected with an Introduction by
JACOB E. VAN VLEET

ORBIS BOOKS
Maryknoll, New York 10545

ORBIS BOOKS
Maryknoll, New York 10545

Fathers and Brothers
MARYKNOLL

Founded in 1970, Orbis Books endeavors to publish works that enlighten the mind, nourish the spirit, and challenge the conscience. The publishing arm of the Maryknoll Fathers and Brothers, Orbis seeks to explore the global dimensions of the Christian faith and mission, to invite dialogue with diverse cultures and religious traditions, and to serve the cause of reconciliation and peace. The books published reflect the views of their authors and do not represent the official position of the Maryknoll Society. To learn more about Maryknoll and Orbis Books, please visit our website at www.maryknollsociety.org.

Copyright © 2016 by Jacob E. Van Vleet

Published by Orbis Books, Box 302, Maryknoll, NY 10545-0302.

All rights reserved.

Pages ix–xi represent an extension of this copyright page.

No part of this publication may be reproduced or transmitted in any form or by any means, electronic or mechanical, including photocopying, recording, or any information storage or retrieval system, without prior permission in writing from the publisher.

Queries regarding rights and permissions should be addressed to: Orbis Books, P.O. Box 302, Maryknoll, NY 10545-0302.

Manufactured in the United States of America

Library of Congress Cataloging-in-Publication Data

Names: Ellul, Jacques, 1912-1994 author. | Van Vleet, Jacob E., editor.

Title: Jacques Ellul : essential spiritual writings / selected with an introduction by Jacob E. Van Vleet.

Description: Maryknoll, NY : Orbis Books, 2016. | Series: Modern spiritual masters series | Includes bibliographical references.

Identifiers: LCCN 2015042320 | ISBN 9781626981836 (pbk.)

Classification: LCC BX4827.E5 A25 2016 | DDC 230/.42--dc23 LC record available at http://lccn.loc.gov/2015042320

Contents

Acknowledgments

For his enthusiasm and assistance with this project, special thanks to Robert Ellsberg at Orbis Books. It has been an honor to edit a volume in the Orbis Modern Spiritual Masters Series and a delight to know that Jacques Ellul is now a part of it, alongside like-minded prophetic voices such as Thomas Merton, John Howard Yoder, Leo Tolstoy, and William Stringfellow, among others.

For countless hours of conversation about Jacques Ellul, and for their constant encouragement over the years, I would like to thank J. Peter Escalante, Eric Gerlach, and Robert Abele. Also, many thanks to David Gill, president of the International Jacques Ellul Society, for organizing a trip to Bordeaux and Trièves in the summer of 2015. On this visit we were able to meet with Ellul's children, Jean, Yves, and Dominique, as well as distinguished friends and followers of Ellul. Discussions with Daniel and Anita Cérézuelle, Daniel Compagnon, Patrick Troude-Chastenet, Simon Charbonneau, Jérôme Ellul, Jeff Shaw, Lisa Richmond, and David Lovekin were particularly enlightening and inspiring. To all these I am deeply grateful.

Finally, I am especially indebted to my wife Moriah for her countless hours of reading and editing, and for her ceaseless optimism and spirit of hope.

Sources and Abbreviations

ABR   *Apocalypse: The Book of Revelation.* Translated by George W. Schreiner (New York: Crossroad, 1977).

AC   *Anarchy and Christianity.* Translated by Geoffrey W. Bromiley (Grand Rapids, MI: William B. Eerdmans, 1991).

EF   *The Ethics of Freedom.* Translated by Geoffrey W. Bromiley (Grand Rapids, MI: William B. Eerdmans, 1972).

HQ   "Innocent Notes on the 'Hermeneutic Question.'" In *Sources and Trajectories: Eight Early Articles by Jacques Ellul That Set the Stage,* edited and translated by Marva J. Dawn (Grand Rapids, MI: William B. Eerdmans, 1997).

HTA   *Hope in Time of Abandonment.* Translated by C. Edward Hopkin (New York: Seabury, 1972).

HW   *The Humiliation of the Word.* Translated by Joyce Main Hanks (Grand Rapids. MI: William B. Eerdmans, 1985).

IYSG   *If You Are the Son of God: The Suffering and Temptations of Jesus.* Translated by Anne-Marie Andreasson Hogg (Eugene, OR: Cascade, 2014).

LF   *Living Faith: Belief and Doubt in a Perilous World.* Translated by Peter Heinegg (San Francisco: Harper & Row, 1983).

MC   *The Meaning of the City.* Translated by Dennis Perdee (Grand Rapids, MI: William B. Eerdmans, 1970).

MF "The Meaning of Freedom According to Saint Paul." In *Sources and Trajectories: Eight Early Articles by Jacques Ellul That Set the Stage*, edited and translated by Marva J. Dawn (Grand Rapids, MI: William B. Eerdmans, 1997).

MP *Money and Power.* Translated by LaVonne Neff (Downers Grove, IL: InterVarsity, 1984).

ND *The New Demons.* Translated by C. Edward Hopkin (New York: Seabury, 1975).

PK *The Presence of the Kingdom.* Translated by Olive Wyon (New York: Seabury, 1967).

PM *Prayer and Modern Man.* Translated by C. Edward Hopkin (New York: Seabury, 1970).

PR "Political Realism." In *Sources and Trajectories: Eight Early Articles by Jacques Ellul That Set the Stage*, edited and translated by Marva J. Dawn (Grand Rapids, MI: William B. Eerdmans, 1997).

RB *Reason for Being: A Meditation on Ecclesiastes.* Translated by Joyce Main Hanks (Grand Rapids, MI: William B. Eerdmans, 1990).

SC *The Subversion of Christianity.* Translated by Geoffrey W. Bromiley (Grand Rapids, MI: William B. Eerdmans, 1986).

TWTD *To Will and to Do: An Ethical Research for Christians.* Translated by C. Edward Hopkin (Philadelphia: Pilgrim House, 1969).

VR *Violence: Reflections from a Christian Perspective.* Translated by Cecilia Gaul Kings (New York: Seabury, 1969).

WIB   *What I Believe*. Translated by Geoffrey W. Bromiley (Grand Rapids, MI: William B. Eerdmans, 1989).

Introduction: The Presence of the Kingdom in an Age of Violence

In a 1964 journal, Thomas Merton wrote, "I am going on with Ellul's prophetic and I think very sound diagnosis of the technological society . . . It is some comfort to find someone who agrees with my position."[1]

Merton is among a broad list of leading thinkers who have been influenced by Jacques Ellul. From Christians to atheists, anarchists to politicians, artists to activists, the array includes such figures as William Stringfellow, John Howard Yoder, Ivan Illich, Ursula Franklin, Vernard Eller, and even Theodore Kaczynski (*the Unabomber*—who adopted Ellul's critique of technology, while utterly ignoring his wider moral perspective). While some of these names may at first seem surprising, together they signal Ellul's truly dialectical and interdisciplinary worldview, which is embodied in his own canon.

Of the over fifty books he wrote in his lifetime, most were either sociological or theological. Ellul referred to these as "two rails of a train track," both moving in the same direction but separate and distinct. For nearly every sociological book he wrote, Ellul would write a theological or spiritual counterpart. For example, Ellul's sociological work *The Political Illusion*, an analysis of modern politics, was soon followed by its spiritual counterpart, *The Politics of God and the Politics of Man*, a study of political power in 2 Kings.

While acknowledgment of this contrast is vital to understanding Ellul, this book is a compilation of writings from his spiritual side. Rich with uncommon and remarkable wisdom, this portion of Ellul's volumes is undeniably timeless, yet is especially apt in today's landscape. Of course, this collection is by no means exhaustive, but its selections reflect Ellul's essential and imperative message: one of profound spiritual observations and ultimately of hope.

BIOGRAPHY

An only child born in Bordeaux in 1912, Ellul grew up with an awareness of the paradoxes of human existence even as a young man. His father, an Italian Serb, was a firm agnostic and skeptic. His mother, French–Portuguese, was a devout Protestant. Ellul's father was often distant with Ellul and emphasized the virtues of duty and honor over compassion. Conversely, his mother was quite affectionate and loved poetry, art, and music. Ellul would go on to inherit and embody many of his parents' admirable qualities.

Ellul's family was poor, and his father was often out of work. His mother taught art lessons at home to make ends meet. As a child, Ellul wanted to be a naval officer, but his father pushed him to study law. Ellul began to study at the University of Bordeaux in 1929 and completed his doctorate in 1936 with a dissertation on ancient Roman law. Throughout his university years, Ellul stood out as an exceptionally bright student and won a number of academic distinctions.

When Ellul was in his late teens he had a dramatic and life-changing conversion experience. He was always hesitant to discuss the event in detail, but he described it briefly as

> *overwhelming, I would even say violent. It happened during the summer holidays. I was staying with some friends in Blanquefort not far from Bordeaux. I must have been seventeen at the time and I had just taken my final exams at school. I was alone in the house busy translating Faust when suddenly, and I have no doubts of this at all, I knew myself to be in the presence of*

*something so astounding, so overwhelming that entered
me to the very center of my being . . . No words were
uttered. I saw nothing. Nothing. But the presence was
unbelievably strong. I knew with every nerve in my body
that I was in the presence of God.*[2]

Over the next several years, Ellul would struggle with this incident. His conversion was ultimately a gradual process. Only when he realized that faith was not to be confused with dogmatic religion, and that faith could bring freedom, was Ellul persuaded. And later, when studying the works of Karl Barth and Soren Kierkegaard, his faith became concretized.

Around the same time of his conversion to the Christian faith, Ellul encountered the writings of Karl Marx. This convergence would prove to be nearly as influential for Ellul as his encounter with Christianity. As his family's poverty prevailed, Ellul's father increasingly relied on him to help provide for the household. Throughout his teen years, Ellul tutored Latin, French, Greek, and German for income. This financial pressure greatly influenced Ellul's later political views. It also created fertile ground for Ellul's encounter with Marx. He recalls this experience:

*I remember my father spending days looking for work.
Given his abilities, I felt that it was an absolutely stupefying, incredible injustice that a man like him was unemployed; that he had to go from company to company,
and factory to factory, looking for any job at all and
continually getting turned down . . . Then, in 1930, I discovered Marx. I read* Das Kapital *and I felt I understood
everything. I felt that at last I knew why my father was
out of work, at least I knew why we were destitute . . . As
I became more and more familiar with Marxist thought,
I discovered that it was . . . a total vison of the human
race, society, and history.*[3]

Marx's thought would become a lifelong component of Ellul's sociological and theological hermeneutics. Ellul once described his life as being captivated by Marx, on the one hand, and the Bible, on the other—two foundational pillars that provided Ellul with a solid intellectual and spiritual grounding for his pursuit of a more just and egalitarian society. In particular, Marx's critique of the unbounded pursuit of money and material goods, and his longing for a return to a simpler way of life are ideas found throughout Ellul's work. Also mirrored in Ellul's writings is the criticism of alienation and illusion created by modern political and economic institutions. After he became a professor, Ellul would teach a yearly course on Marx, which was always one of the most popular courses among the students. More importantly, however, Marx made a profound and lasting impact on Ellul in this way: "it was Marx who convinced me that people in the various historical situations they find themselves, have a revolutionary function in regard to their society."[4] This notion, according to Ellul, always remained a central component of his own life and scholarship.

During his time studying law at university, Ellul was greatly influenced by Bernard Charbonneau (1910–96). Ellul first met Charbonneau in secondary school, and they remained lifelong friends. Charbonneau, an agnostic, would deeply affect Ellul's view of politics and society. It was through Charbonneau that Ellul would come to the conclusion that the primary source of exploitation and alienation in the modern world is technique. (As we will see, Ellul defines technique as the modern technological milieu within which we live, and at the same time, an overly calculative mind-set that worships power, politics, and technological progress.)

In the 1930s, Ellul and Charbonneau encountered Emmanuel Mounier (1905–50) and the personalist movement. Personalism emphasized the liberation of the individual over the increasing control and bureaucracy of the state. Its adherents rejected fascism of all strains and encouraged members to form small groups of like-minded individuals in resistance to authoritarianism. Following the contours of Marxist thought, Mounier believed that a revolution of sorts was needed in order to regain personal freedom. However, unlike Marx, Mounier maintained that an essential component of effective revolution was a renewed spiritual consciousness. These ideas influenced Ellul significantly, and one can readily find them throughout his spiritual writings.

In 1937, Ellul married Yvette Lensvelt. They met at university when he was a doctoral student and she was a first-year law student. Lensvelt had been raised a Catholic but had become disillusioned with the faith, and was swayed by Nietzsche by the time she and Ellul met. However, her curiosity about the Bible was sparked upon seeing Ellul read it, and she expressed her interest to him. From then on, the two would study the Scriptures together throughout their lives.

They had three sons: Jean, Simon, Yves, and a daughter, Dominique. In 1947, Simon passed away at the age of six: a devastating event that would pain the Ellul family—especially Yvette—for years to come. Ellul and his wife would remain married until her death in 1991. In his own words, "She helped me to learn how to live . . . she also taught me how to listen . . . she changed my whole way of being."[5]

After receiving his doctorate, Ellul took his first teaching position in Montpelier in 1937 and the following year accepted a post as a lecturer at the University of Strasbourg. When the Vichy government took over France, Ellul was fired from his position at Strasbourg for speaking out against the Germans and the Vichy regime. Ellul and his family immediately fled to the outskirts of Bordeaux to escape persecution. They lived in a small community, farmed, and aided the Resistance. Ellul's assistance was in the form of hiding Jews, refugees, and Resistance fighters. He also provided many with false papers, helping individuals move in and out of the country.

While Ellul never engaged in violent acts of resistance against the Vichy regime, he voiced his sympathy toward those who did.

Even at this early stage in his life, he embraced the path of non-violence. However, Ellul worked diligently in his fight against fascism, even when this meant aiding those who took up arms against Marshal Pétain's authoritative state.[6] With his family, Ellul spent four years living in support of the Resistance until the Liberation of France in 1944. They then moved back to Bordeaux where Ellul joined the faculty at the University of Bordeaux. He also briefly took a political position as a council member and deputy to the town mayor, but quickly retreated from government involvement under advice and urging from his wife and Charbonneau.

From 1946 until his retirement in 1980, Ellul held the positon of Professor of the History and Sociology of Institutions, as well as Professor of Political Studies. Ellul remained committed to Bordeaux and to engagement with his local community, alongside his success as an academic. He firmly believed that one of the foremost tragedies of the modern age was the loss of community, family, and face-to-face relationships. For this reason among others, Ellul chose not to uproot his family to pursue professional or economic interests. (In fact, Ellul is believed by some to have coined the phrase "Think globally, act locally," one of his favorite sayings.[7])

The majority of Ellul's life after the war was primarily one of teaching, researching, and writing. He penned more than fifty books on history, sociology, and theology. He also published hundreds of essays in books, magazines, and academic journals.

In addition to his demanding university post and academic work, Ellul spent many years working with troubled youth in his community. In the late 1950s, Ellul's friend Yves Charrier began an organization for homeless youth and street gangs. Soon Ellul became involved in Charrier's Prevention Club and acted as a legal advocate; counselor; and, for a short time in the 1960s, a Bible teacher. Regarding his work with the youth, Ellul stated, "It is not young people who are maladjusted to society but our society which is maladjusted to human beings."[8] He firmly believed that technological and bureaucratic societies led to alienation, addiction, and violence. This belief was confirmed as Ellul continually witnessed violence against youth in his community by means of the state bureaucracy, the judicial system, and the living conditions of life on the street. Ellul advocated one-on-one work with the troubled youth of his community as the only viable solution to the inherent violence in society. He continued this work until the late 1970s.[9]

Ellul was involved in the French Reformed Church to a greater or lesser degree throughout his life. Early on, Ellul was active in local Reformed organizations and societies. In the late 1960s however, he became increasingly skeptical of anything *institutional*, including denominational churches and establishments. This attitude primarily grew from Ellul's distaste of modern politics, which he believed to be mirrored in many religious institutions.

One of the last straws came in 1973, when Ellul campaigned for the French Reformed Church to encourage and support conscientious objectors and promote a complete rejection of military power and control. Ellul's proposition was refused, confirming his conviction that the church was no longer motivated by the authentic gospel, but rather by its own political interests.[10]

Though Ellul was skeptical and critical of institutional Christianity, he was a strong advocate of personal Bible studies and home churches.[11] In fact, throughout Ellul's life he led Bible studies in his home and encouraged others to do likewise. Ellul believed that a more genuine and personal type of Christianity could be embraced and propagated in this way: an organic and grassroots community of faith rather than hierarchical, top-down religion.

Ellul's anti-institutional approach to faith was motivated in large part by the Danish philosopher, Soren Kierkegaard (1813–55). Ellul had a longtime interest in Kierkegaard's life and writings. Kierkegaard's philosophy, often referred to as Christian existentialism, had a deep and lasting influence on Ellul's interpretation of Scripture and Christianity in general. Kierkegaard emphasized the need for believers to live out the faith rather than turn it into a dogmatic system of rules and strictures. The goal of Christianity, according to the Dane, is to enter into a direct and personal existential relationship with God, and then to practice one's faith in a concrete and practical way. Christianity, at its heart, is not an empirically objective or scientifically logical belief system for Kierkegaard. It is instead a deeply personal experience with God, and it must be lived and practiced. Ellul inherited this existential understanding of the faith, along with Kierkegaard's skepticism of religious institutions and dogma.

In addition to Kierkegaard, Ellul credited the Swiss Reformed theologian Karl Barth (1886–1968) as a centrally important influence on his theology. In particular, Ellul was deeply impacted by Barth's continual emphasis on the radical otherness and mysteriousness of God. As a young convert to Christianity, Ellul had begun by reading the works of the Protestant reformer John Calvin (1509–64), whose writings Ellul felt were suffocating to the mystery of the Christian faith. Barth's theology, in contrast, embraced the unknowability, unpredictability, and radical freedom of God. For Barth, as for Ellul, God can never be forced into a theological or scientific box but is completely free to do as God pleases—even if this means acting in ways that do not conform to empirical or natural laws.

Once Ellul read Barth, he was launched onto a new spiritual path and he abandoned Calvinism. Though he remained within the French Reformed Church, Ellul stayed closer to the Christian existentialism of Kierkegaard and the thought of Barth. However, as the reader will become aware, Ellul cannot be categorized easily. He was constantly bucking tradition, speaking out against political and religious institutions, and infuriating those on both the right and the left. He did not care about theological correctness or doctrinal orthodoxy as such. His emphasis, following Kierkegaard and Barth, was on becoming one with God, embracing God's mysteriousness, and living out one's faith as the *presence of the kingdom* on earth.

Throughout his life Ellul continued to challenge and criticize systems of power. He pointed out the similarities and parallels between capitalism and totalitarianism. He strongly condemned the Vietnam War, racism, and the immense social and political propaganda created by the United States. He spoke out against the fetishization of technology, warning of an ominous society where individuals willingly become automatons and drones. Ellul's life was one of the social critic and prophet, or as he put it, the "perpetual protester."[12]

LIVING FREELY IN A WORLD OF NECESSITY

Ellul spent his life examining the Christian's place in a modern world increasingly dominated by technology, war, propaganda, and suffering. His primary concern was to awaken people to the consequences of what he called *technique*. The primary and most vital (and perhaps most misunderstood) theme throughout Ellul's work is *technique*. Ellul generally uses this term in two different ways. First, technique refers to the accumulation and domination of technologies, which surround and envelop all human activities. Second, technique is a blindly adopted mindset that strikingly mirrors technology. This consciousness—as Ellul sometimes calls it—strives for efficiency, control of others and nature, and views all people and the earth as a means rather than an end. Through the lenses of technique, we see others and ourselves as mere instruments or as pieces of technology that can be used for a practical purpose. More and more, people unknowingly espouse this way of understanding the world. This leads to the devaluation of nature and all living things—human and nonhuman. Subsequently, Ellul contends that people become psychologically and physically alienated from themselves, from their loved ones, and from God. Technique is a sphere of necessity. That is, one who lives in any modern civilization will *necessarily* be enveloped by the world of technology and by an instrumentalist mind-set. Ellul firmly believes that technique has saturated every sector of society—politics, economics, education, science, religion—and that it is impossible to escape. This permeation restricts the freedom of the individual and leads to despair. However, Ellul argues that there is a second sphere within the domain of technique: a realm of freedom and hope, which he called the realm of the spirit.

In Ellul's spiritual writings, he continually calls on Christians to open themselves up to the mysterious voice of God. Through this openness, individuals can escape the realm of technique and live in freedom. Only then, living in the domain of the spirit, can one experience freedom of thought and action, as well as the liberty to reject the values of technique, particularly the value of human power. The selections of Ellul's writings in this book will illuminate and expand on this hopeful exhortation.

NONVIOLENCE AND THE VIOLENCE OF LOVE

From his days of resistance to the Vichy Regime, Ellul remained an advocate of nonviolence. Ellul believed that two primary types of violence dominate in the modern world: physical and psychological. The first involves destruction or harm of one's bodily well-being, whereas the second—namely, propaganda—involves controlling people by using fear and manipulation. Both kinds of violence, according to Ellul, destroy the inherent human capacity to freely grow, create, flourish, and love.

Paradoxically, while violence robs us of our freedom, it is often carried out in the very name of freedom. Ellul reminds us that propagandists administer their psychological abuse by using emotionally charged words like *liberty* or *happiness* in order to win the support of the masses. Meanwhile, ruinous military invasions persevere under the guise of effectuating democracy or justice.[13]

Ellul argues that we need to recover the biblical notion of justice, which not only includes the love of one's enemies but also the protection and advocacy of the poor, the ill, and the oppressed. "[The early church] seems to witness to the teaching of Jesus on the level of personal relations—Love your enemy, turn the other cheek. Jesus carried the commandment 'Thou shall not kill' to the extreme limit, and in his person manifested nonviolence and even nonresistance to evil."[14] The majority of early Christians rejected the use of violence, including their refusal to participate in the military until the fourth century. After the rise of Constantine the Great (272–337 CE), the church promoted participation in the military, and it was only then that Christians (in significant numbers) did so.[15]

Ellul encourages today's Christians to look back to the first three centuries of Christianity, when the teachings and actions of Christ were considered the essential guide to life. Jesus refused to engage in violent behavior, even to his own detriment. In the imitation of Christ, early Christians did not excuse violence or military behavior; they stood opposed to it, and they refused to compromise.

Ellul points to various reasons for our current temptation to resort to violence. First, in an age so permeated with the corporate media and its convincing but often fallacious messages, many Christians become persuaded by social and political propaganda. Rather than responding to social issues through a reflective and authentic faith in God, one accepts and adopts the narrow perspective presented by news outlets. One hears, for instance, that a military solution is the only answer to a conflict and unquestioningly agrees. Sending our troops and dropping bombs are accepted as rational first responses to any number of worldwide issues. Peaceful, democratic solutions are rarely discussed or mentioned—and soon they are forgotten. Yet Ellul argues that Christians must not become numb to combative actions, even when they are our society's first answer.

The second reason violence is an attractive temptation is because it is often believed to be the most efficient answer to a particular problem. Ellul argues that the spirit of the world is one of power, and power manifests itself in a fetish for efficiency. In our fast-paced society, then, we always seek that which is most efficient: the newest technology, the quickest path between two points, the speediest method. Thus, psychological and physical violence are usually seen as the quickest solution to crime and injustice. Meaningful dialogues and educational approaches are not even considered as answers; they would take far too long. Instead, quick and forceful acts of violence are chosen, be they bullets fired by law enforcement or sugar-coated lies told by politicians. For Ellul, these *solutions* represent the mind-set of technique in their quest for efficiency and desire for power—and the spirit motivating these violent acts is antithetical to the spirit of Christ.

Ellul defends nonviolent anarchism as the only legitimate Christian political position. In his book *Anarchy and Christianity* (1988), he explains, "There are different forms of anarchy and different currents in it. I must say very simply what anarchy I have in mind. *By anarchy I mean first an absolute rejection of violence.*"[16] (Further passages from this thoughtful work follow in this anthology.)

Ellul expands this definition to include a complete refusal of power and domination. Political and religious power, in Ellul's view, are only gained and maintained through the use of psychological and physical violence. In contrast, he reminds us that Jesus acted as a servant and never strived for domination, and was therefore an authentic anarchist. Ellul argues that Jesus's followers should mirror the anarchistic method of Jesus by resisting quick solutions to societal problems and by rejecting violence and standing up against it—even when this is the most arduous option.

Clearly, Ellul sees violence as tactically irrational and inefficacious, and this stance does not stem solely from his biblical worldview. He maintains that if anyone—atheist or believer— carefully and objectively observes the violent methods employed by various law enforcement institutions—military, courts, police—one will see that violence works only for the destruction of liberty and democracy. Whether physical or psychological violence is used, truth, freedom, and even human lives are sacrificed for the sake of efficiency. Yet with the rise in unfettered technological growth and broadening consumerism, it is impossible to live in a world without violence. As newer military technology is produced, it will be purchased and employed. Moreover, violence is fed by the values of competition and speed, which are themselves inescapable in the modern world.

In spite of this inevitability, Ellul believes that we can recognize our dilemma and respond justly. He explains that we

> *must struggle against violence precisely because, apart from Christ, violence is the form that human relations normally and necessarily take. In other words, the more completely violence seems to be of the order of necessity, the greater the obligation . . . to overcome it by challenging necessity. This is the fixed, the immutable, and the radical basis of the Christian option in relation to violence.*[17]

To carry out this mandatory opposition to violence, Ellul encourages Christians to engage in what he calls the violence of love. While this may at first sound contradictory to Ellul's rigid stance against all violence, he explains that the violence of love is, in fact, the opposite of other violence: it is life affirming, it selflessly looks out for others and never oneself, and ultimately—as Paul put it—it seeks to overcome evil with good. Ellul explains,

It is not the violence of terror or coercing but the vio-
lence that makes us . . . insistent in our demand that the
other live . . . the other cannot be compelled to be fully
human except in and through absolute love . . . [This]
certainly does not mean having rights over the other in
any way, being one's boss, one's tutor, one's guide, one's
counselor; it means urging one forward with the vio-
lence of love that never seeks its own advantage, never
seeks to possess or dominate.[18]

This is not only the path of Jesus; it is also a rare stance
that directly opposes the values of our highly competitive,
efficiency-worshipping society.

THE PRESENCE OF THE KINGDOM

Ellul reminds us that humanity is now constantly confronted
with necessity and fatality, bondage and death. In response, the
authentic Christian is called to "break the fatality which hangs
over the world"—and with God's grace, can do so through three
primary tasks.[19] Fittingly, Ellul uses biblical language to name
these three pursuits, the first of which he described as being the
salt of the earth. As a visible sign of the new covenant, the Christian should display in his or her speech, actions, and indeed, his
or her entire life, what the new covenant represents: the preservation of our relationship with God through Christ. There is no
better way of doing this than to work diligently for the better-
ment of one's own community—especially for the exploited and
alienated.

Christians are also to be the light of the world. The primary
mode of dispelling darkness is to speak out against ubiquitous
myths and idols. Ellul explains that this not only drives out
meaninglessness and fatality, it also makes it possible for Christians and others to see clearly. This clear vision, in turn, brings
clarity of purpose, hope, and authentic significance to history.
Without this light, purpose and meaning in life are lost.

Finally, Ellul maintains that Christians need to fulfill the task of living as sheep among wolves. Like Christ, who gave his life for others, so too must Christians be willing to sacrifice themselves for the sake of the world. The essential difference between sheep and wolves is that the latter seek to dominate and control. Sheep, on the other hand, submit to the will of God and live peacefully without struggling for power. In a *survival of the fittest* society, it is not surprising that the mentality of the wolf dominates. Still, says Ellul, we must imitate Christ and his service to God and others. Only then will we fulfill all three of the tasks of an authentic Christian.

However, Ellul warns that this is not an easy or flawless path. He elaborates, "The Christian cannot consider oneself pure, as compared to others. The Christian cannot declare that he or she is free from the sin of the world. A major fact of our present civilization is that more and more sin becomes collective, and the individual is forced to participate in collective sin."[20] Because we must often comply with the behavior of our larger society, we are participants—whether explicitly or implicitly—in its wrongdoings, and this is only furthered by globalization. We support unethical working conditions by purchasing necessary commodities that are often the only ones made affordable or available to us. We often have no choice but to pay into our government's invasions and wars, even when we have no part in these military decisions. As it becomes exceedingly difficult to live a moral life in a highly interdependent society, we must be honest with ourselves and remember that we are all participants to a greater or lesser degree.

Once this inescapable sinfulness is realized, Ellul warns us that two primary temptations immediately arise. The first is for Christians to want to disassociate with the non-Christian world, separating themselves from society and avoiding all appearances of sin in the world. This temptation, however, contradicts two fundamental functions of what a Christian is to do: be salt and

light. Ellul urges the Christian to not dodge his or her responsibility, but to be in the world, living out the faith in a public,
unapologetic manner.

In addition to being lured by isolation, the Christian is tempted
to undertake what Ellul calls the moralizing or Christianizing of
the world. We see this often in society: Christians condemning
the immoral behavior of non-Christians and calling for them
to adhere to Judeo–Christian ethical standards. But expecting
others to see the world through the lens of the Christian worldview will never work. According to Ellul, modern secular society
exists in a fallen state of futility. Within these conditions, and
without the grace of God, nonbelievers can never be expected to
adhere to a Christian ethic. Instead of trying to force and project their morals onto others, Christians must be the light, salt,
and sheep of the fallen world, primarily by resisting violence
and refusing to bow down to the modern idols of technology
and political institutions. By doing this, Christians can shatter
the world's hopelessness and meaninglessness, and become the
presence of the kingdom—the body of Christ on earth. Ellul
describes this task:

> *I believe that our vocation on earth is to establish a*
> *harmony that includes all that we call justice, liberty,*
> *joy, peace, and truth. Our vocation is to set up harmony*
> *between people, between earthly things, between the ele-*
> *ments that compose our universe. This is why all arro-*
> *gance, all desire for domination, and all our attempts to*
> *exploit other things or beings run contrary to our voca-*
> *tion.*[21]

CONCLUSION

Christians, as the *presence of the kingdom*, bring freedom into
a world bound by necessity. This freedom can only be harnessed
and appropriated by refusing to worship the values of technique:
efficiency, power, and material accumulation, among others.

Ellul's hopeful message is that Christians can introduce a real and enduring influence into the sphere of necessity. No longer is it obligatory to engage in a struggle for power, to participate in violent acts, or to strive for money. Instead, Christians must embrace the violence of love, which is service to God and others. Only then will authentic and lasting freedom ensue.

ABOUT THIS VOLUME

Both sides of Ellul's work—sociological and theological—are related in a dialectical way. Like Karl Marx, who understood history as being comprised of clashing forces, Ellul, too, viewed history as being pushed forward by the continual tension between the force of technique, on the one hand, and the force of the spirit, on the other. Ellul's two veins of writings mirror this dialectical tension.

In this work, I have collected key passages from Ellul's specifically Christian writings; I have not drawn from his sociological books or essays. In addition to the themes I have mentioned, Ellul's spiritual writings emphasize hope, the love of God, universal salvation, and hearing the spoken word rather than falling prey to the visual idols of the modern world. This volume has been arranged around all of these essential topics.

Ellul was a systematic writer, although he was sometimes rather repetitive. It is my hope that the clarity and poignancy of his words will provide readers with a helpful introduction to his thought and might spark an interest in Ellul's books themselves.

As a final note, I have taken the liberty to occasionally correct spelling and punctuation for the purpose of clarity. I have also altered Ellul's writings to be gender inclusive. I have no doubt that Ellul would have approved of these minor changes, as he encouraged his readers to continually find ways to reformulate language so as to better communicate the hope of the Christian message.[22]

NOTES

1. Thomas Merton, *Dancing in the Waters of Life: Seeking Peace in the Hermitage (The Journals of Thomas Merton)*, ed. Robert E. Daggy (New York: HarperCollins, 1997), 161, 326.

2. Patrick Troude-Chastenet, *Jacques Ellul on Politics, Technology, and Christianity: Conversations with Patrick Troude-Chastenet* (Eugene, OR: Wipf & Stock, 2005), 52.

3. Jacques Ellul and William H. Vanderburg. *Perspectives on Our Age: Jacques Ellul Speaks on His Life and Work* (Toronto: House of Anansi Press, 1981), 5.

4. Ibid., 11.

5. Troude-Chastenet, *Jacques Ellul on Politics, Technology, and Christianity*, 93–94.

6. Ibid., 67.

7. See Randal Marlin, *Propaganda and the Ethics of Persuasion* (New York: Broadview, 2003), 34.

8. Quoted in Andrew Goddard, *Living the Word, Resisting the World: The Life and Thought of Jacques Ellul* (Carlilse, Cumbia, UK: Paternoster, 2002), 49.

9. See ibid., 48–50.

10. See ibid., 43.

11. Two excellent volumes of Ellul's home Bible studies have been compiled, edited, and translated by W. H. Vanderburg. See Jacques Ellul, *On Freedom, Love, and Power* (2010), and *On Being Rich and Poor: Christianity in a Time of Economic Globalization* (2014), both published by the University of Toronto Press.

12. Troude-Chastenet, *Jacques Ellul on Politics, Technology, and Christianity*, 107.

13. See Jacques Ellul, *Propaganda: The Formation of Men's Attitudes* (New York: Knopf, 1965).

14. Jacques Ellul, *Violence: Reflections from a Christian Perspective*, trans. Cecelia Gaul Kings (New York: Seabury Press, 1969), 9.

15. Similar arguments are made by John Howard Yoder in *The Politics of Jesus* (Grand Rapids, MI: Wm. B. Eerdmans, 1972) and by William Stringfellow in *Conscience and Obedience* (Waco, TX: Word Books, 1977).

16. Jacques Ellul, *Anarchy and Christianity*, trans. Geoffrey W. Bromiley (Grand Rapids, MI: Wm. B. Eerdmans, 1991), 11. Emphasis added.

17. Ellul, *Violence: Reflections from a Christian Perspective*, 127–28.

18. Ibid., 166–67.

19. Jacques Ellul, *The Presence of the Kingdom*, trans. Olive Wyon (New York: Seabury Press, 1967), 11. These three tasks are described in *The Presence of the Kingdom* and in various other of Ellul's spiritual writings.

20. Ibid., 13.

21. Jacques Ellul, *What I Believe*, trans. Geoffrey W. Bromiley (Grand Rapids, MI: Wm. B. Eerdmans, 1989), 51.

22. See Jacques Ellul, "The Problem of Communication," in *The Presence of the Kingdom*, 96–136. See also Jacques Ellul, *The Humiliation of the Word*, trans. Joyce Main Hanks (Grand Rapids, MI: Wm. B. Eerdmans, 1985), 264–67.

1

God and Jesus

Throughout Jacques Ellul's spiritual writings, he primarily referred to God in one of three ways: Wholly Other, Love, or Trinity. Ellul placed a strong emphasis on the unknowability and radical otherness of God; it was important to him to point out our human inability to know God without the aid of God's revelation.

He also continually emphasized the all-encompassing love of God, maintaining that love is God's most fundamental attribute. This is quite evident in Ellul's constant reference to God and Jesus as liberators who bring freedom and salvation to all humanity and the earth.

Ellul held a strong commitment to the belief that the most adequate way of understanding and speaking about God is through the Trinity. (In fact, Ellul preferred to call himself a Trinitarian rather than a monotheist for this very reason.) His emphasis on the Trinity was a result of his fundamental belief that the constituents of reality are essentially dialectical and paradoxical, and that the Trinity embodies these constituents perfectly.

Surpassing his other descriptions of God, Ellul places the greatest weight on the individual's direct and existential encounter with God. Ultimately this relationship cannot be fully expressed in human language or symbols, says Ellul. Rather, it must be lived out through love, compassion, and the refusal to bow down to today's idols. Jesus was the exemplary model of this lifestyle.

GOD'S SECRET PRESENCE

I believe in God's secret presence in the world. God sometimes leaves us in silence, but God always tells us to remember. That is, God recalls us to the word which God has spoken and which is always new if we rebuild the path from the word written to the word lived out and actualized. God is a God incognito who does not manifest in great organ music or sublime ceremonies but who hides in the surprising face of the poor, in suffering (as in Jesus Christ), in the neighbor I meet, in fragility. We need to lay hold again of the elementary truth that God reveals God-self by the fleeting method of the word, and in an appearance of weakness, because everything would be shattered if God revealed Godself in power and glory and absoluteness, for nothing can contain God or tolerate God's presence. God cannot be known directly but only through that which is within the realm of human possibilities. This is why imposing ceremonies and ornate basilicas are absurd. Solomon recognized this in his prayer at the dedication of the temple: "Behold, heaven and the highest heaven cannot contain thee; how much less this house which I have built!" (1 Kings 8:27). There then follow the intercessions of Solomon for the poor, for aliens, for the hungry, for sinners, and for suppliants. In all these situations of our human weakness God comes to us. But we can be sure that in our situations of wealth and power and domination and expansion and high technology and unlimited growth God is not present. God tells the rich that they have their reward; why then should they have God as well? This is why God is silent in our western world of opulence and technology. God is certainly present, as in the rest of the universe. But God is present incognito and in secret. God is present as God was when the serpent spoke to Eve and she was enlightened about the tree and took the fruit in order

to be as God. God is present incognito and has enough respect
to allow the creature to choose its own destiny after issuing a
warning.   —*WIB*, 148–49

GOD AS WHOLLY OTHER

My first reflections revolve around the central conviction that
I cannot have a single coherent image of God. I cannot say at
a given moment that God is simply this or that for me. God is,
but God is also other things at the same time which may finally
be the opposite. I cannot attempt a synthesis or reconciliation
between the different elements in what I believe I can understand about God. I thus renounce here any attempt at intellectual coherence.

In my thinking there are three different levels. The first is that
of what I have learned intellectually about God, the result of the
work of theologians and the evolving consensus of the church.
Jesus is the incarnation of God, true God and true man. God is
the Creator. God is Three and One. God reveals Godself progressively. God intervenes in history. God creates new heavens and
a new earth. There is nothing original here, but it corresponds
to a great truth. I am aware of the linguistic problems that arise,
but they do not trouble me. Most of the questions that are put
on the matter are false questions. As for the rest, we are wrong
to think them new. The problem of the adequacy of language
has harassed theologians from the very first, as we see from the
debate between Eunomius and Gregory of Nyssa or the dispute
about universals. We have made few innovations, and the formulation of the thinking of the church has gone on in spite of all
the difficulties. We cannot presume to set aside the knowledge of
God handed down by the church. Nor can we have the feeling
that it is of no direct concern to us today. Arguments that suggest
as much, for example, the anthropomorphism of its definitions,
their strictly cultural character (inasmuch as they express the
beliefs of a given culture that another culture cannot assimilate),

or their dependence on this or that philosophy, seem to me to be weak and superficial. Without going into detail, I would simply say that after serious and profound study of all these critical systems, I have concluded that none of them is convincing or can sway my own convictions. To want to change a name or representation is of little interest. To say that we must not think of God up there because God is down here is simply to ask for a change of signpost. To talk of the ultimate or the unconditioned (which seems to me to be exactly the same thing as the classical ingenerate) is no doubt not incorrect, but it is also no more true than to talk of the eternal or the absolute. I thus accept with little difficulty the teaching of church fathers and theologians, at least those who have produced the traditional teaching of the church.

But can I stop there and receive this deposit of the faith (in spite of the scandal this formula represents today) as adequate and well packaged? For two reasons I have to say, not that everyone was wrong up to the present day, nor that this way of thinking about God is historically outdated, nor that it is idealistic and hence does not concern us, but that I cannot stop there and merely accept it. My first reason is simple: if God is God, God obviously cannot be totally known or circumscribed or put into a human formula. There is always something more to know and understand and receive. All theologies and all knowledge of God will always fall short. It is a commonplace of theology that the finite cannot contain the infinite. My second reason is different: if God is the God of Jesus Christ, God demands of me a personal decision because God has set up a personal relation. This personal decision presupposes action on my part, including intellectual action. I cannot spare myself the trouble of facing up to this revelation of God, of trying to express in my own way what this personal relation to God entails. Not being wholly satisfied with what the church's tradition teaches about God, I have to go my own way and try to think out the question for myself.

Concerning the second level of reflection upon God, I am at once inhibited by something that many theologians have come up against, and this is perhaps because I belong to my age and setting. The point is that if God is God, I cannot know anything about God on my own, and even less can I say anything about God. God is the Wholly Other. If God were not, God would not be God. If God is, I cannot even conceive of what is at issue. Since my process of acquiring knowledge is tied to what is familiar, God is truly unknowable. I have neither the right nor the ability to manipulate God in such a way as to be able to know God.   —*WIB*, 169–71

GOD'S LOVE

Once and for all we must finish with humankind's absurd pretension to fathom the mysteries of God's will. If God is truly God, God is outside the reach of our intelligence; if God is truly God, our intelligence can never grasp anything but a falsification of God's true nature. "Who are you to answer back to God?" But in the precise details of this revelation given us of God, we can, in any case, perceive one astonishing thing, and that is the patience of God's attention and love for humankind . . . And for Christians, this love is *too* well known, since they think they know Jesus Christ. Now it is true that the center of God's love is in Jesus Christ, but it is also well to understand that God's love reaches everyone's life. God in God's love, because God *is* love, takes into account one's will, takes into account one's desires and one's maddest intentions, understands one's wildest revolts, takes into account all one's endeavors. God does not want to save an abstract person, but you and me, each individual in their unique particularity. God did not love humankind abstractly in Jesus Christ, but every crushed and miserable unique soul in the midst of the wandering crowd. And God has kept God's records throughout history. Certainly not an account of merits and demerits, of sins and good works. All that has already been taken care of in the pardon streaming from the cross . . .

This is the path God has chosen, and we have but to follow its shining traces through history. But because Christ is Savior and Lord of both creation and humankind, Christ is also Savior and Lord of humankind's works. In Christ, God adopts the individual *and* their works. God tolerated it through the world's history and now God has taken charge of it. God has chosen to dwell in it. And just as the individual living in the city is directly subject to the spirit of the city, now those who dwell in it are in communion with God, for God has truly assumed it in the most classical meaning of the term, and has transfigured it. For even in the resurrection, God does not shatter human hopes. Rather, God fulfills them there. And on the other side of death, in God's new creation, God renders to humankind the setting they preferred.

But God renders it to humans in Christ; that is, in the new creation, all that Christ came to accomplish is finally realized. Direct communion with God is reestablished, so there is no more temple or church. Uncorruptible, immortal life again belongs to humankind. The balance of creation is re-created when Christ, after uniting all things in himself, hands everything over to God. And all this happens in the New Jerusalem, so as to forever link human work with Christ's. In this city, the adventure of Christmas is totally realized and finds its culmination. The human version of the incarnation finds an eternal home. This is the very heart of this extraordinary manifestation of God's love.

—MC, 174–75, 177

THE TRINITY

The Trinity is really the distinctive characteristic of Christianity. One God indeed, but the great objection of Jews and Muslims to Christianity is that it is not strictly monotheistic, since in their view Christians worship three Gods. From the days of the church fathers, theologians have debated endlessly in an attempt to reconcile the oneness of God with the threeness of the Trinity (one God in three Persons). But if we lay primary stress on

monotheism, we forget that the revelation in Christ is primarily
Trinitarian. The stakes are serious, for to stress monotheism is
to make Jesus Christ secondary. But if we maintain that Jesus
Christ alone reveals who God is, that he alone teaches us the love
of God, that he alone is the image of God, that he alone makes
a covenant between God and us, that he alone is our salvation
through his death, that he alone is our hope through his resurrection, that he alone is the truth, then other monotheists regard
us as polytheists. If we want to engage in a pleasant dialogue, if
we want to appear to be people of goodwill, if we are ready for
agreement on a common basis, we shall have to set Jesus Christ
aside. We shall just have to stop being Christians. The Trinity
is not a matter of theological accommodation to difficult problems. It is not a human invention. It belongs to the very essence
of the biblical revelation. Creation by the Father, the incarnation
of the Son, and transfiguration by the Spirit are the architecture
of revelation. Moltmann was right when he even went so far as
to say that monotheism engenders authoritarianism and totalitarianism both ecclesiastically and politically. Trinitarian thinking ensures at the same time both divine and human liberty.

—*WIB*, 177–78

JESUS: THE TOTALITY OF THE WORD

Christian thought radicalizes transcendence, the total break
between God and the world, which can be healed only by the
incarnation, on the basis of which no development of the sacred
is possible. The Christian God makes Godself known in Jesus
Christ and not elsewhere. (I refer to what was affirmed in the
first century, in the first three or four Christian generations:
primitive Christianity.) Outside Jesus Christ, God is totally
unknowable and inaccessible. As I have said before, the only
possible theology relative to God is what much later (from the
twelfth to fifteenth century) will be called negative theology;
that is, declaring what God is not. There is no possibility of saying positively what God is. This means that the condemnation of

the visible in the religious domain receives emphasis. There can be no demonstration of either the divine mystery or God's revelation. The Christian God is a *hidden* God. Nor can any image of Jesus be preserved or imagined. We have here a religion of the Word alone, and Jesus is himself the totality of the Word, living and not ritualized.

—SC, 59

JESUS AND THE REJECTION OF POWER

Twenty years ago, when there was a debate about nonviolence, I was the first to stress that what characterized the action of Jesus in his life on earth was not nonviolence. Indeed, we all know how his indignation boiled over against the merchants in the temple. From this incident some theologians even inferred that he did not reprove revolutionary violence, so that they were ready to direct the action of the poor against wealthy merchants. We are also all aware of the violent charges Jesus hurled against the scribes and hypocritical Pharisees, against the rich, against Chorazin and Bethsaida, etc. What constantly marked the life of Jesus was not nonviolence but in every situation the choice not to use power. This is infinitely different. Not using power is not weakness. Weakness means inability to do what I would like to do or ought to do. Not using power is a choice. I can, but I will not. It is renunciation. This general and specific decision not to use power does not rule out occasional acts of violence. But this violence is an expression of brutal conflict, whereas the nonuse of power is a permanent orientation in every choice and circumstance. Power is there, but one refuses to use it. This is the example set by Jesus. The consideration that the omnipotent God, in coming among us, decides not to use power, is one of the most revolutionary imaginable . . .

But this permanent orientation of Jesus, this express choice not to use power, places us Christians in a very delicate situation. For we ought to make the same choice, but we are set in a society whose only orientation and objective criterion of truth

is power. Science is no longer a search for truth but a search
for power. Technology is wholly and utterly an instrument of
power; there is nothing in technology other than power. Politics
is not concerned about well-being or justice or humanity but
simply aims at achieving or preserving power. Economics, being
dedicated to a frenzied search for national wealth, is also very
definitely consecrated to power. Our society is the very spirit of
power. The main difference from previous societies is that they
also undoubtedly sought power but did not have the means to
achieve it. Our society now has the means to achieve unlimited
power. Thus we Christians today are placed in the most difficult
of all situations. We have to repudiate both the spirit of the age
and the means that it employs. If we do not, if we yield even a
fraction to these forces, we will betray Jesus Christ just as surely
as if we committed some individual and limited sin. For this is
a choice for life (nonviolence being part of it), and no other is
possible. Pretending that we can express the Christian faith in
works of love (aid to the poor and sorrowing, etc.), or in revolutionary acts to achieve justice, is treason if we engage thereby
in the use of power. For the last word of love is that never in any
circumstances will it express or indicate power in relation to
others. Today only a nonuse of power has a chance of saving the
world.   —*WIB*, 149–51

THE SUFFERING SERVANT

I have said that we need to take into consideration the most
humble suffering of Jesus. The Gospels often speak of it. For
example, Jesus was hungry. We are told this explicitly after Jesus
fasted in the desert for forty days (Matthew 4:2). In another
text, when Jesus is confronted with so many requests (and especially requests for healing), hunger is alluded to: "Then, because
so many people were coming and going that they did not even
have a chance to eat" (Mark 6:31). On another occasion, when
Jesus arrived at Bethany for his final journey to Jerusalem, Mark

tells us that he was hungry (11:12). Of course, in each of these instances, the purpose of the text is not primarily to inform us that he was hungry. However, we should not neglect this detail, nor should we dismiss his cry of "I am thirsty" during the crucifixion (John 19:28). John tells us that these words were spoken so that all Scripture might be fulfilled. Granted, but let us not forget that at that very moment, like any crucified person, he was actually thirsty. So of course, he experienced this human weakness—to be hungry and to be thirsty—and *genuinely* did so. Let us now pause and consider the first thought.

We know from the experience of people who have gone on hunger strikes that forty days of fasting is the limit of what a person can bear. Of course, some will say (and as I myself have written on several occasions) that the number forty is symbolic. Yet, for the remainder of the passage to make sense, there must have been some concrete reality making Jesus very hungry. It is indeed immediately after this that the devil appears to him and tempts him by suggesting that he transform stones into bread. Obviously, the Jesus whom the Gospels describe could have worked that miracle and thus could have had plenty of bread. It is important for the Gospel writer to remind us that Jesus was *really* very hungry. Otherwise there would have been no temptation. Jesus was really tempted on this most humble physical level. He was hungry. This reminds us that Jesus experienced all the temptations arising from physical needs, just as any person does.

Jesus refuses to perform this miracle. It is his first refusal to perform a miracle. Why does he refuse? Was it because the suggestion came from the devil? As I have stated before, the devil is not a person in my understanding. Rather, the temptation comes from the fact that Jesus is experiencing an urgent need to eat and that he commands power that would enable him to satisfy his hunger. In fact, Jesus sees in this temptation to perform a miracle an action of the "dia-bolos" the one who separates, the one

who would have separated him from God. Why? This is because
if he had performed the miracle, it would first of all have been
a miracle performed *in his own interest*. Jesus never performed
miracles *for himself* because he came to bear witness to a love
for which he will sacrifice himself.

He will never use his power for himself; quite the contrary,
where he is concerned, he offers himself up in non-power. Furthermore, this miracle consisting of turning stones into bread
would have been a typical example of the *marvelous*. We see
many times that Jesus never gave in to the "pleasure" of doing
marvelous things. The miracles of Jesus have nothing to do with
the works of magicians, sorcerers, and so on . . . They *all* come
from his love of others and of God.   —*IYSG*, 19–21

THE THREE TEMPTATIONS OF JESUS

We must now start with the three temptations reported in Matthew 4:1-10, Mark 1:12-43 (accounts without any comment),
and Luke 4:1-13. I have already written about these three temptations on several occasions, but how could we leave them aside
when they first of all contain all the other later temptations and
secondly are most relevant to our times.

The first remark I would like to make—and which is essential—is that the Spirit leads Jesus into the desert (the Holy Spirit,
says Luke). Mathew's affirmation is more serious: he is led into
the desert to be tempted. The desert is the traditional place
where "spirits" dwell, the place where the scapegoat is sent, and
the place of trial par excellence. We have said that God does not
tempt us or force us to undergo temptation. Sometimes, however, God sends us into temptation. Jesus was brought by the
Spirit into the desert *in order to* be tempted by the devil there.
Is Jesus aware of this "in order to"? It is unimportant; he goes
where the spirit leads him. He subjects himself to the very conditions that will give rise to the trial: he fasts for forty days, which

is reminiscent of the forty years Israel spent in the desert as well as Elijah's forty days. He is weakened by this first trial.

When the devil, the separator, comes to him, he is a weakened man who is not at the height of his powers. Is that important? Certainly. "God chose the weak things of the world to shame the strong." The devil is certainly strong. And if Jesus wins, it is not because he is in great "athletic" form or at the height of his powers. I can already hear the protests of some readers: "If Jesus wins?" But, if he is God, how could he not win? We certainly have a decisive question here; it is of the same order as the question about his death on the cross: because Jesus is God, he *could* not have *died*. Or some will say, "He knew that he would rise from the dead." Therefore, there is no "real" death. We must absolutely reject these statements. For if he is God, he did not fool us, did not pretend. Otherwise, his death and all of his life would have been a colossal fraud, a mockery. No, although he was God, he was as fully tempted as any person (but with what higher risk!), and he really did die in the horror of abandonment.

If Jesus wins, it is by the sheer grace of God and his complete responsibility. But Jesus could have lost. He could have let himself go. He could have accepted such reasonable propositions. For let us remember that Jesus did not meet a character with wings and horns who began a dialogue with him! There is *no one* facing him . . . only himself. The questions and the suggestions that come to him are only coming from within. He is asking those questions of himself. They are so reasonable! And the moment is tragic. If Jesus wins and rejects the temptations, he wins *nothing but* a life of grief and toil, a life of renewed temptation all the way to the cross. And if he loses, if he obeys one of these reasonable propositions, he wins everything on earth . . . But then, God would have lost everything; this is because the final means chosen by God to show God's love to all human beings would have been lost just like the previous ones! What a great risk there is in this bet, which is the opposite of the wager presented by the philosopher Blaise Pascal.

Bread

After a forty-day fast, Jesus is hungry! The simple thought that comes to him is inevitable: Why not transform the surrounding stones into bread? Why not perform a miracle? He will perform so many of them! And perhaps the question springs up in his mind: if I really am the son of God, it is possible. It would be some kind of proof that he could give himself. Thus far, there had only been legends from his childhood or an illusion at the time of his baptism . . . After all, why would Jesus not have needed additional certainty? God has indeed sent me, and I am indeed his Son, the Messiah . . . These are not blasphemous questions since no one has ever been able to explain the co-existence of the "two natures." The issue is to prove that he is the Son of God by performing a miracle. We will find this temptation throughout the Gospels, but it is usually men who are asking for the proof. Here, we begin with a question that contains all the subsequent questions. We are warned that whenever Jesus is faced with this question, it will be because the devil is speaking through one person or another. Yet, in itself, this proposition seems quite normal. A man is hungry; if he is able, why would he not find the bread needed to satisfy this basic need? We are forced to expand upon this and understand the proposition in its broadest sense. To satisfy a need—and here the need in question is *obvious,* that is, the most pressing hunger—calls into question the totality of modern civilization in its frenzy of production and consumption. Elsewhere, I have called this first temptation the economic temptation. The legitimization of all our activity, of all our inventions, and of all our production is that they satisfy our needs. As long as we can declare that if "we put a product on the market, it is because there is a corresponding need," anything can be justified. It is obvious that nuclear weapons correspond to a need from the military, that cars capable of 155 miles per hour satisfy a need for power, and that VCRs answer a need for constant entertainment . . . We can always invent a new need that did not previously exist but that will appear to be essential as soon as it is possible to satisfy it. Our economic life only exists to satisfy needs that themselves need to be created so that we can sell a new product. Once this need has been created, however, it becomes a *real* need and the absence of satisfaction is painful. It is not quite possible to separate natural needs from artificial ones, for artificial needs become natural ones. It is true that the morphine addict feels as strong a need for morphine as any person feels for food. The only difference is that the little newborn baby has a need for food and no need at all for morphine. The latter only becomes a need through the physiological manipulation caused by the use of morphine: it exists before the need. Certain needs only appear with the products that are required to create them.

I believe this brief story is all about our economic life. And of course, the devil had predicted the consequences: as soon as people were able to make these fantastic machines, they thought they were God. This characterizes us: we are really divine because we have transformed these materials, these substances, these natural elements, into elaborate products that can satisfy unimaginable—and truth be told—unknown needs. This particular judgment that "We are divine" is found in many places such as in cults of personality, the commemoration of important historical movements, the obscure writings used in Christian initiations, and the arcane texts laboratories produce, as well as the declaration so often heard these days: "I have *faith* in humanity." Of course, we should! Through the miracle of productivity, people have indeed *proven* that they are divine!

Faced with all this, Jesus refuses to perform this miracle of demonstration—even though he is hungry—and instead lays down a corner stone: "Man does not live by bread alone, but by

every word that proceeds from the mouth of *God*." The hunger
for bread is unquestionable. But hunger for the word of God—
felt less obviously in the belly—is even more essential. He is not
only saying, "I refuse to perform this miracle because I refuse
to prove that I am the Son of God," but also "I—and all other
people—hunger *first* for the word of God." This is not about
denying hunger for food or the usefulness of providing bread
to the starving, nor is it about producing what is really necessary for a person's life. It is about discovering that the word of
the living God, the Being of all Beings, the Father, is even more
indispensable to a human life *worthy of humans*—for in reality,
the production of all our innumerable "goods" lowers people
beneath that which is human.

Power

The devil is not vanquished, for he immediately offers another
proposition, a more subtle one, which will become a temptation.
I will follow the order of temptations in the Gospel of Luke
rather than the Gospel of Matthew because it seems to me more
coherent. "The devil led him up to a high place [a very high
mountain according to Matthew] and showed him in an instant
all the kingdoms of the world. And he said to him: 'I will give you
all their authority and splendor, for it has been given to me and
I can give it to anyone I want to. So if you worship me, it will all
be yours.' Jesus answered: 'It is written: "Worship the Lord your
God and serve him only"'" (Luke 4:5-8). After the "economic"
temptation, we now have the "political" temptation.

The first and very harsh pronouncement made by this text
concerns precisely "the essence of the political." I have already
made use of it in my studies of the State. The devil's declaration
is very firm: political power in all the kingdoms, political glory,
and political greatness all belong to the devil. This is of course
very serious! Of necessity, this leads us to consider governments
and powers in a different light. They are all emanations of Satan;

they have all given allegiance to the devil; and they have all been received from the devil. This is true of the institution itself as well as the person who holds power at any particular time. The very famous saying that "Power corrupts, and absolute power corrupts absolutely" is both rooted in and explained by this text. Furthermore, this is not an unfathomable mystery: Who *wants* to wield power? Who *wants* to take advantage of political glory? Obviously, it is the person who is already possessed by a spirit of power. One "gets into politics" to satisfy one's will to power. The politician's discourse on "the public good" and his or her explicit devotion to the cause of humanity and so forth are all smoke screens about the reality of power itself and about all politicians. Our text is very harsh: those seeking political authority must not only be indwelt by the spirit of power but, what is more, must *worship* the one who can give this power—the devil, the tempter. Beyond him, such people must worship power itself. We can therefore say without hesitation that all those who have political power—even if they use it for good ("the devil also knows how to do good at times")—have received it through the devil and are, even if they are unaware of it, worshipers of *diabolos*. If this is the case with the proposal that the devil makes to Jesus, how could we believe that other individuals would be more unscathed than Jesus! But let us always remember that this thirst for power is only one particular expression of covetousness. Since Adam, it has been the keystone of all human maliciousness and voraciousness.

Yet one point must be made: Why is this temptation offered to Jesus by the *diabolos?* This will enlighten us as to the reality of the political! We have said that the *diabolos* is the one who divides. Is this not precisely what characterizes all politics whether it be from the left or the right, whether it be fascist or Marxist? Politics *divides*. It sets people against one other and classes against one other. It lays down theories and dogmas that create barriers, and the more politics claims to be "unifying" the more it divides. Without politics and political leaders, people would be able to agree and understand one other; but as soon as politics intervenes, they engage in all sorts of battles. So it is perfectly normal that the *diabolos* should offer power!

Religion

We now reach the third temptation in ascending order (according to Luke, for it comes second in Matthew). This time, the devil changes tactics: since Jesus countered him with Torah, he will now use it too. The devil knows the text of this revelation. This should alert us. Our very use of the Bible belongs to the realm of temptation! It is not enough to know the Bible or to use it appropriately and find the text that would suit us. Why does Jesus not obey the text?

This is all the more strange because when the devil uses this text, he acknowledges implicitly that Jesus is the Son of God. "He will command concerning you." He only asks him to prove it, to attest to it with certainty. There is, however, some progress since the first instance of the devil's saying, "If you are the Son of God . . ." Of course, this is not the first example in the Gospels of "demons" recognizing in Jesus, the Messiah, the Son of God— but Jesus commands them to be quiet. Here, the temptation that he will often face is more severe and is founded on revelation.

How often have we used these texts in search of approval or justification or proof that we are indeed "Christians" and that our conduct conforms to the will of God? Here is precisely the first limit: *to use* the biblical text. That is, instead of listening and obeying, we try to justify *ourselves* by using the revealed text. Each time we use it in this way, we can be certain that we have fallen into temptation. Or when in a discussion, we use such and such a text to draw an argument from it. The Bible is neither a collection of recipes nor a collection of arguments. But there is something more serious: the devil uses the Bible to bring Jesus to the point of breaking away from his Father. Yet, these texts do exist and they are actually taken from this Bible. So what can we say? This is where the question of interpretation arises—after the question of our use of the Bible. The great rule is that no text, no verse, and no declaration can stand by itself. To separate a text from the totality of God's revelation will inevitably cause us to distort it. There is in fact a double separation that we must avoid: first of all, and this is a classic error, there is the separation of a verse or a sentence from its text, from its context. When we argue that it is possible to make the Bible prove "anything," we are perfectly correct if we separate a sentence from its context. The second separation is even more serious, however: it is to separate a text—which always refers to God or to the action of God—from the revelation of God and about God as a whole, as it is given in the *whole Bible*. In other words, we must study the text together with all of God's action in history, with God's people Israel, and in Jesus Christ. Hence, there is a precise and rigorous limit to the interpretation of a text: each one can only be received and understood in relation to all the others and to all that we know about God through them (this is interpretation according to the analogy of faith).

Here, the devil takes one text—which is true, which is indeed from Scripture, and which is indeed about the Son of God—but he completely distorts its meaning by making what would be a miracle attesting God's love for the Messiah, for God's Son, into some sort of demonstration-miracle, a miracle of the marvelous. This is precisely the kind of miracle that Jesus always refuses to perform because he would not accomplish the will of his Father at all if he fulfilled this prophecy for his own profit and were to appropriate it! That for which the devil asks is a miracle to prove that Jesus is actually the Son of God. In fact, however, Jesus came for the forgiveness of sinners and certainly not to "impress the crowd." In his work, he can only ask for faith ("Blessed are those who have not seen and yet believed"), and if the relationship to God the Father is a relationship of love and faith, the relationship to the Son is necessarily one, too. There are thus no proofs. Even less will he grant what the devil wants since he is the antithesis of love. The devil wants a miracle of sheer power: to leap from the pinnacle of the temple and not be injured. Jesus will always refuse to perform miracles in order to prove or convert or to show his power, *except* when his power is at the service of his love . . .

We have now discussed the three fundamental temptations that people can know: the economic temptation, the political temptation, and the ideological-religious temptation. These are the three domains in which humanity wants to assert its power and ensure its autonomy and its greatness.

—*IYSG*, 58–64, 67–69, 70

2

The Role of the Christian

According to Jacques Ellul, we live in an age dominated by increasing technocratic rule, violence, and the loss of human freedom and dignity. More than ever before, Ellul believed that today's Christians need to embrace hope and spread its message. This is to be the main emphasis of the modern Christian kerygma, even prior to faith. It is only once hope is embraced that the believer can authentically pray, make meaningful changes in the technocratic realm, and live out his or her faith in freedom.

Hope, prayer, faith, and love are all dialectically intertwined and interrelated. Together they direct the role of the Christian and bring freedom into our present sphere of necessity and bondage.

PROCLAIMING HOPE IN AN AGE OF ABANDONMENT

We have here the central question for preaching, for evangelization, and perhaps for the entire Christian life today. We persist in centering all on faith, on believing or not believing. Now, for the present, the accent has shifted. It is placed on hope, on living with or without hope. Modern humans are said to be no longer capable of faith, no longer suited to belief. It is said that our modern world does away with faith, and that it is no longer

possible to believe what used to be believed in the creedal statements of a former age—but what a mistake!

Never have people believed as much, everything and nothing. The modern world is above all else a religious world. It is
loaded with religions—communism, Maoism, nationalism, revolution—all are purely and specifically religious attitudes. The
modern world is not really secularized, in spite of all the absurd
ballyhoo based on a whole series of misconceptions, and on
an extremely superficial analysis. This is essentially a world of
the sacred. The political enemy is "damned." Wars are ideological wars, that is to say, wars of religion. Social movements are
sacred. Revolution is an act of God. Technology belongs to the
domain of the sacred, and science even more so. The most that
can be said is that modern humans have completely desacralized
the natural environment, they have transferred all the sacred to
the cultural and the social. One need only observe the entranced
state of those who talk revolution, or the complete irrationality of discourses on politics, irrespective of the specific question
under discussion. The modern world is overflowing with myths.
It is constantly producing myth, but they are no longer *the same*
myths as before, and they no longer come by the same process.
This contradicts the superficial view that humanity, attached to
ancestral forms of myth, is being demythologized. We are caught
up in the development myths (and those of underdevelopment),
in the myths of self-management and growth, as well as in the
myths of fascism and imperialism. World and humanity are
crammed with faith, with religion, with belief, with mythology.

If the debate were on the question of the transmission of the
Christian faith, the obstacle confronting us would not be that
of reason and science, but rather, the multiplicity of "faiths."
In any case, it is quite inaccurate to ask, "How witness to the
faith in a rationalized, secularized world?" To keep insisting on
that is a waste of time. It is a display of blindness on the part
of the church and of theology, and it is a second proof of the

abandonment in which we find ourselves. The question could very well be, "How witness to the Christian faith in the midst of all these beliefs and these new myths?" I do not look upon that question as totally useless.

In other words, I think that the warfare of faith should continue, in fact, to be waged against the idols and the false gods. I believe that Christ the Lord has to be proclaimed anew in the face of all the lords of this world, and that the struggle is as radical today as in the days of the primitive church. But with regard to helping humans and finding an answer to their anguish, longing, and misfortune, it is not the proclamation of faith which is decisive, but the proclamation of hope. . . .

Only the deep need of humanity today drives me to say that the center of the Christian message now is hope. Furthermore, this is not an "exchange of values" which I am proposing! It is not because preaching about faith answers any problems and no longer sinks in, nor because the preaching of love has failed and I am falling back on the third choice, on the line of retreat. I am not reaching for a consolation prize, nor making a desperate attempt to recover something which might possibly work. Certainly not. If I were convinced that before God, within the command of God, it were necessary to continue preaching conversion and revealed truth, no prior failure, no battle to be fought, would make me hesitate.

I am led to opt for hope by quite another route. If it is true that the world in which we live is a world of abandonment, if it is true that God is silent and that we are alone, then it is under these circumstances and at this moment that the preaching, the proclamation, the declaration, and the living of hope is urgent. It must be prior and central. —*HTA,* 78–79, 82–83

HOPE AS CRITICISM OF HUMAN POWER

When I was saying that humanity advances by hope in all the domains that God seems to abandon by God's silence, the diametric opposite was implied. It is not a question of any domain of power and effectiveness. As far as power is concerned, exactly nothing has changed since Genesis. When we take into consideration the actual facts of human power, how could we be so absurd as to turn the biblical myths upside down? Human power is always a consequence of the break with God. It is always the deed of Cain, of Babel, of Nimrod, and of Mammon. There is no other. It is the demonic pride of putting oneself in God's place, of hunting God down and vanquishing God. It's always characterized by blood, murder, and the degradation of women, by the triumph of money and power. I know that in writing this I am going counter to the contented purring which justifies the "greatness" of modern humans, but what can I do?

Torture, exploitation, dictatorship, and the universal destruction of nature constitute the essence of the power of humans. The blind sycophants ignore fact. They ignore the concrete reality of the facts as well as the internal structure of the phenomenon. When they talk about a valid step forward for humanity in replacing God, they comprehend nothing of what is happening, that it is not humans who are taking the step forward but the technological system and the system of state control, both of which expand in autonomous obedience to their own laws of growth and give humans the appearance of success!

Hope, a sally into the territory abandoned by God, is the contrary to all this. It is the calling into question, not of God but of the power of human beings. If it is hope, it is "by nature" that which plays upon an "unachieved-unachievable." It is not fulfilled by the methods of power. It does not actualize itself either by techniques or by administration. It is hope precisely because its purpose surely cannot be attained by the instruments of power. What the powers of humans achieve is in no sense the object of hope, for the very reason that it can be attained through the internal logic of the system.

Hope does not rejoice over the fact that God is leaving us free to act. It wants, to the contrary, to have a pole of reference which is God. It demands that God speak, because without the presence of the God, who is the Wholly Other, the Almighty, and the Lord, humans can only go from disaster to chaos. There no longer is any light or any way. Hope is the negating of the powers and successes of humans, since it cannot be fulfilled except by God's presence with humans . . .

Yet it actually advances to root out God from God's turning away. It advances into the unknown territory which God abandons to it. It advances into the Word of God which is dead and done with. It advances into the past works of God in order to find there a recovery of strength. It advances into the desert of the church (not to reform it, but to draw from it a witness of the Spirit). It advances into the devastation of the world in order to make worn-out humanity go forward, to get humanity (humans, not the system to which humans have surrendered) to take one more step. It advances into the inflexible, the morbid, and the frenzied in order to catch there the unlooked-for, the unsuspected, which would give evidence that God still is not entirely absent.

Hope is on the lookout for every sign. It cannot accept the conclusion that God is gone, that God is dead, and that humans are abandoned (while calling themselves grown-up). It advances into God's territory and, if necessary, replaces God's Word with the echo of its own word. It occupies the places to which God has to return, to which it will ultimately force God to return. It is the march toward, the march into, that promised land, but without God any longer to lead the way and do the work. All illusion to one side, this march toward and into the promised land is one that hope alone can make us continue.

—*HTA*, 212–14

HOPE AS PRAYER

Prayer is the sole "reason" for hope, at the same time that it is its means and expression. Prayer is the referral to God's decision,

on which we are counting. Without that referral there can be
no hope, because we would have *nothing* to hope for. Prayer is
the assurance of the possibility of God's intervention, without
which there is no hope. Prayer is the means given by God for
the dialogue with God, that is to say, it is the very junction of
the future with eternity, where we have seen that our hope is
located. In its dialogue it embraces the past presented for pardon, the future defined by the cooperation between the praying
person and God, and eternity, which prayer lays hold of through
the sighs uttered by the Holy Spirit.

Without such prayer we can piece together a few false hopes
to give the appearance of hope, but all that, even when arranged
theologically, can only be illusory. That is why it is quite right
to recall that hope is based on God's promise constantly fulfilled
and renewed. But how can we forget that, throughout the Bible,
this promise is linked with the ceaseless outcry of prayer? It is
human prayer which demands the fulfillment, and it is again
human prayer which demands its renewal and its ongoing. Without prayer, the promise and its fulfillment are forces just as indifferent and blind as *Moira* (fate) and *Ananke* (necessity).

So without prayer there is no true promise, since there is no
one either to receive the promise or to take it seriously. However,
just as prayer is prerequisite to the promise (for the promise to
become promise!), so it is not the promise which incites one to
prayer. Also, since there is no longer any joyous liberty of the
person turned toward God, since our general sterility ignores the
value of an outpouring, since our rationalism turns our eyes into
microscopes and points us to the ground (the moon is another
ground, now that we have walked on it), since our efficiency
forbids our adding faith to these stammerings, since our gravity
prevents our play of free speech toward God . . . where are we
to get the meaning, the urgency, and the need for prayer today?

Very well, I was led to the conclusion that if we have every
reason for not praying, we have just one reason only for praying,

namely, God's command. There is no need to look for other explanations or foundations. Prayer today is no longer a spontaneous motion of one toward the creator, nor of a ransomed soul toward one's redeemer, nor of the person destined for death and for life toward the one who resurrects. It can strictly be nothing other than obedience to a requirement which has credence as such, and here there is no need to go into profound analyses and exegesis. Either faith leads me to acknowledge that there is *a* command, and that at the center of that command is an instruction to pray, or else there is no faith.

But if I engage in prayer, then hope is born. If I live hope, I think only of hope in prayer. The two feed on each other. The moment that happens, the question about faith and its content becomes a thing of the past. The act of prayer, a pure obedience without an end in sight, resolves both the problematics of faith and all the impossibilities of human hope. —*HTA*, 272–74

HOPE AS PERSEVERANCE

The person of hope is a person of a demanding, wide awake (the two things inextricably go together: "Watch over us" is constantly being said), tensed waiting, which does not let itself be diverted or taken in, either by the game of the serious things of politics, economics, technology, and science, or by the seriousness of the games of eroticism and philosophy, art and leisure. Stubborn, firm, unassuming, the person of waiting rushes into the dark of God's silence and of the abandonment. This person has a stature over and above those who hurry about in their automobiles and their unions. This one has chosen another field of battle, and this person knows that it will be as a result of one's own combat that all the rest will get its meaning and its possibility. This person openly rejects the action constantly being proposed, in favor of the waiting for the moment when all will have become possible again. This person concentrates all one's forces on this waiting, which is in itself a concentration of forces, through its silence and its avoidance of scattered action.

This waiting is decisive, since we should know that nothing will come to pass without it—nothing. There is no return, no Kingdom, if we fail to live in this fervor of eyes lifted up to the hills awaiting our help, the fervor of the watchman, trembling with fear, awaiting the dawn.

Still we have to realize that these promises of God are not fulfilled mechanically nor arbitrarily (according to a plan fixed from all eternity, or according to a whimsy of God). The promise is fulfilled every time in connection with a person who has bet one's whole life on that promise, that is, in the expectation of its fulfillment. I have often written that it is of the very foundation of the last things that Jesus is coming again, that the true motif is not our forward motion *toward* these last things. It is the motif of these last things *in* our history. Except that the eschaton does not speed our way on rails. There is no automatic, mechanical movement comparable to the onrush of time. There is no capricious coming of Christ similar to a return from a journey (obviously, the parables of the return are not to be taken literally!). The Kingdom comes, and Christ comes again, through the person who waits with unmitigated hardness, with a demand without loopholes, with an exalted fervor, and with a persistence which refuses to be diverted by anything. The Kingdom comes and Christ comes again through that person alone, but not *for the person's sake* only. It is for the sake of all, as the prophet watches for all.

The treason of Christians and of the church was to settle in, to wait contentedly for something for which one hoped less and less, to organize so as to wait as comfortably as possible, and finally no longer to expect anything at all, but to put oneself to sleep in the feverish activity of organizing society, the world, the economy, and of discovering science. In that terrible time God continued to speak. God pressed God's appeal. God kept up what was no longer anything but a monologue, so that there were two disconnected monologues. Now it is abandonment . . .

So we have to choose our actions and decisions, not only in relation to the personal, social, and moral context, but in relation to this eschatological reality. In that way, and only in that way, can we say that our works tend to actualize the Kingdom of God we are hoping for, tend to render it present in our midst. Now this action, which is marginal, disquieting, off-center, eccentric, anachronistic, and timeless (if it is not *all* of that, it is not expressive of the waiting), can only be begun endlessly over and over again with perseverance. It is an indefinite waiting, an inexhaustible perseverance. The epistles refer to it often! (Romans 5:3-8; 15; Ephesians 6:18; II Thessalonians 1:4; Hebrews 6:12; James 1:3), yet theology and preaching pay scarcely any attention to it! Perseverance, as a quality of the waiting, is one of the tangible aspects of hope. It is hope's response to failure and suffering. It is constancy in the inner life, and it is action in the face of appearances to the contrary, in spite of the refutations thrown at us by facts and events, by the state, by science, by technology and by history, by all the gods.

Perseverance never counts on success, on a possible outcome. It is not because the situation might get better that one keeps on going. To the contrary, perseverance completely repudiates all the success-criteria of action. This is decisive, for we are not hoping for any success, but for the return of Jesus Christ and the establishment of his reign. The return and the Kingdom are indissolubly linked to our tangible acts, but these have no need of a present success, that is, they have no need to attain their rational objective in order to have their own meaning, in order to be successful when Jesus Christ comes. Here again, as is the case with nearly all action taken in accordance with biblical instruction, there is a disengagement of the action from its "rational-concrete" effectiveness, since the reference of the action is not to the obtaining of a result. It is either obedience to a command

or a waiting for the return. Consequently, we should be able
to keep on indefinitely renewing these acts, economic, political,
cultural, etc., without receiving the slightest human satisfaction
or encouragement.   —*HTA*, 261–62, 266–67

HOPE AS REALISM

I have attempted to demonstrate elsewhere that realism is the
fundamental attitude of the Christian toward the world, and
that its intellectual rule is one of the foundations of ethics. We
come upon it again here, linked with hope indissolubly. Realism
is characteristic of the pessimism of hope in the exact degree we
have seen. This hope never consists in thinking that things will
work out. Hope can live only in a strict pessimism, but the latter
could bring us to a pessimism for which there is no remedy if we
do not live by hope.

Once again, hope is not something to counterbalance pessimism and realism, to counteract reality clearly seen, understood,
and grasped. Hope finds its substance in realism, and the latter finds its possibility in hope. Without a living hope there is
likewise no human capacity to consider the actual situation.
One can never stand reality. One spends one's time lying to oneself, covering up the real, providing oneself with illusions and
rationalizations. Marx saw this clearly in his theory of the false
consciousness and ideology. He could not have seen it, could
not have attempted to discern the real and to show it to others,
except *with* and *within* a hope. But that hope was deceptive and
insufficient to the degree to which it was purely human, to the
degree to which it was based on historical analysis, and not on
the only possible source of hope. But it must be borne in mind
that Marx's thrust was the only acceptable one, and for that
reason it was the one which made the closest approach possible
to the reality of its time.

Without hope, reality becomes an unbearable mechanism, a
continual damnation, a source of fear and apprehension which

cannot be appeased. One can never look situations squarely in the face, yet one is always frustrated and blocked when one fails to do so. The person who fails to look at the real, to accept it even in its most threatening aspects, to see the impasse or the fatality in which he or she finds oneself, can never find a way out of it either, can never surmount the reality nor in any way get beyond it to make history. It is never the positive and comforting doctrines, the philosophies of progress, the historical or metaphysical optimisms, which incite humans to become human. The doctrine of the "great Yes" given to the creation, to technology, and to humans is a doctrine of stagnation, of systematic opposition to progress and of laissez-faire.

If "primitive" humans had obeyed a "great Yes," had obeyed surrounding nature, they would quite simply have disappeared, wiped out by their foolishness. It was by observing the situation in the most realistic way possible: cold, hunger, wild beasts, and all-around hostility, that humans formulated the great No. "No! I refuse to accept its being that way. I refuse to accept the universe's being one of cold, hunger, and all the dangers." Then, matured by a still unnamed hope, humans acted and won.

Now we are faced with the same choice. That is why hope is still decisive. In fact, only from the standpoint of that hope can we make a decision. But this decision (political, scientific, technological, and economic) only makes sense if it relates to a clear and rigorous view of the real. Without this realism, hope can only fall back into idealism, and it is my belief that idealism, at whatever level, is the worst of all traps, and represents the greatest danger for humanity. . . .

Hope does not begin to *exist* except in the harshness of an expanding implacable force, in the unanswerable nature of the problems confronting the person, in social oppression and mechanization, in the midst of conflict. Elsewhere, one has no use for hope. One gets along quite well without it. All that is needed is to let things go, to leave humans to themselves and let nature

take its course. Hope is power and action only in the presence
of naked reality.

It does no good to tell me that I can never lay hold of naked
reality or that I can only have a cultural view of things and that
pessimism is just as deceptive as optimism, etc. I know that line
quite well. I can say this, that a dead man is a dead man. There is
a reality there, about which it is useless to quibble, which I meet
up with, and which I can do nothing about. It is not a cultural
image. Cultural images are interpretations of this reality after
the fact. The reality itself is grasped and experienced directly.
The moment I begin to examine it, think about it, and interpret it, then yes, I need to be suspicious of cultural images, of
colorplates of interpretation, of my psychological optimism or
pessimism, of my system of thought, etc. But, for one thing, that
in no way changes my experience of the fact, of this raw, given
thing which has put me to the acid test. For another thing, it can
be counteracted by a certain intellectual rigor and by a critical
procedure.

That is why it seems to me that reality is within our grasp,
but that it can only be experienced. There can be no sociology
or psychology without a personal experience of the fact, which
one tries first to grasp and afterward to explain. Hope then acts
to keep the interpretation from being a lie, an illusion, a justification. But more than that, it produces the power whereby we
are not conquered by this reality, whereby the experience of the
death of a person, of a brother or sister, does not bring me to the
point of suicide, or of giving up, but becomes, to the contrary,
the point of departure for life and hope. Yet this realism cannot
be reduced to the purely individual experience of the moment.
I only used that concrete example as a reminder of the fact that
there is a reality outside our artificial representations. Any genuine and usable realism, the kind which will always remain the
necessary condition for hope, has to be defined in its sociological
dimension.   —HTA, 274–76, 278–79

PRAYER AS COMBAT AGAINST DEATH

Thus the act of private prayer is the act through which history is structured in Christ, and it is at this point that the transition from "I" to "We" is inevitable. There is no room for opposition between private, individual prayer and communal, churchly prayer (which is too readily confused with *group* prayer). The most private, informal, and personal of prayers (if indeed we are dealing really with prayer) is necessarily a prayer on behalf of all, since by that act (even if the person praying has no such conscious intention and makes no mention of politics) the history of all takes on meaning and possibility for the future.

Then prayer has its full measure, for we are placed in the midst of the ultimate combat (which is always present) against "nothingness in action." The ancient biblical image for nothingness (the serpent, leviathan), which is always ready to swallow up, corresponds to a reality, both present and final. Only prayer can bring off the victory, and it depends upon us that this victory take place. "For the person who truly prays, the demonic is a horrible dream of incongruity" (Castelli). That is indeed the essential point. Nothingness at work expresses itself in the impossibility of history, in futility, in incongruity (the transient, the unstable, the irresponsible, the disorganized, the nonmoral, etc.). Prayer gives consistency to life, to action, to human relations, to the facts of human existence, both small and great. Prayer holds together the shattered fragments of the creation. It makes history possible. Therefore it is victory over nothingness.

"The God of peace has willed that one person pray for all, just as in one individual God has borne all people" (Cyprian, *De domin. Orat.*, 8). Let us note well that sacrament and preaching lose their import and reality if prayer does not accompany them.

Such is the ultimate meaning of the combat of prayer, in which we discover that obedience in the face of every natural inclination and hope in the face of every probability take on a

value far surpassing our personal concerns. At every moment
the eschatological act of prayer is a combat against death and
nothingness, so that we may pick up once again the thread of
life.   —*PM*, 177–78

PRAYER AS COMBAT WITH GOD

But God does not yield easily. God does not change with every
wind. God does not give in to just any prayer. It is not that there
are good and bad prayers, some pious, good, and proper, while
others are silly, irrational, and heterodox. There are only those
in which one commits oneself from the depths of one's being,
wholly and without reserve, and those other prayers that one
"says," which are deeply emotional but with a feeling different from that of Jesus Christ. There are also ritual and formal
prayers. The combat with God implies the commitment of the
person who is praying.

Here, undoubtedly, we come back to the idea (which we criticized) that the person who prays should carry out what one is
demanding! But that is not the initial aspect of the commitment.
The second aspect is what is involved, just as to love one's neighbor is the second commandment. The first is the commitment
with, for, but we must also add *against* God. One cannot hold
oneself in reserve, one cannot pretend to be aloof in the venture
in which one is asking God to involve Godself fully.

Abraham's prayer goes to the very limit of bargaining and
argument, even to the point of infringing on God's decision.
Jacob's prayer commits all of his strength to the combat: "I will
not let you go." What determination, what violence! The kingdom of heaven belongs to the violent who lay hold upon it, and
let us not talk about "holy violence." It is an extreme and sacri-
legious violence, which is saintly in fact.

But this violence is not accepted by God unless the person
practicing it is ready to bear the shock in return. If God receives
a prayer, the first consequence falls upon the person praying.

Abraham had to submit to the sacrifice of his son as an answer
to his prayer for Sodom. Jacob's thigh was put out of joint, and
he went away lame. However, the most usual experience will be
God's decision to put to work the person who cries out to God.

Yet we must be careful. The pattern is not simple. It is not
merely, "If I pray for bread for the hungry, I must give them
bread," or "I should fight against social injustice," for God's decision is often out of proportion to the prayer, and the answer is
not what is hoped for. When Elijah, in the wilderness, demands,
"It is enough; now, O Lord, take away my life," God answers,
"Arise and eat, or else the journey will be too great for you";
then afterward, "Return to this people and begin your work
again." Also, when Jonah agrees to pay for his disobedience with
his life, God takes him back, to make him do what needs to be
done.

Whoever wrestles with God in prayer puts one's whole life at
stake. Otherwise it would not be a *genuine* combat, or indeed it
would not be a combat *with God*. Whence, though prepared to
give up one's life, one can *only* accept the decision which sends
one elsewhere, wherever God judges best. In the combat in which
the individual has no reservations, God wills also to have no reservations, and if God has already given everything in God's Son,
then God expects one both to take God with complete seriousness in prayer and also to conduct one's self responsibly.

To take God with complete seriousness means to put God to
the test. We never dare enough in petitioning God, in putting God
to the test of what God can do (and of what God has already
wanted to do, since we have the promise). It is not resorting
to magic or uncivilized to demand something of God, as when
Elijah asked that the sacrificial victims be burned, or when Jesus
asked that the fruitless fig tree wither. It is, rather, the audacity
of knowing that God can do that, and of committing oneself
to asking God. It is a commitment of the self, because what a
blow it is if God remains silent! What doubt and what ridicule

can result! If our prayers are prudent and empty, that is because we have become incapable of putting God to the test. We are afraid of risking our reputations. We are anxious about spiritual things, in which we can never be certain of being answered or denied, and we are anxious about good theology (the good being the latest). We treat the demand for a miracle as the mark of a backward, materialistic mind, etc.

In fact, we are afraid, both that God might manifest Godself and that we might be committed unreservedly and without limit. That is the last observation to be made. Whoever enters into combat with God should be aware of the fact that once it is begun it can never be brought to a halt. It has to be pursued to the very end. If a person does not have the courage to go the limit, it is best in that case to stay with the prudent and untroubled request, which has no importance and which guarantees psychological tranquility. The warnings which Jesus gives us apply as well to prayer. To engage in prayer is to perform the basic act of a disciple, and at that moment one is radically alone before God. One finds oneself separated from those nearest, at the same time that one is in communion with them. That is the fulfillment of the saying, "Everyone who has left houses or brothers or sisters or father or mother or children or lands, for my name's sake, will receive a hundredfold." That renunciation is required for the disciple's independence and for the seriousness of prayer (Luke 14:25–33).

So it is important to know whether one is ready to go all the way in the combat and the commitment. God does not tolerate lukewarmness. We must know that genuine prayer is infinitely simple and radically serious. We need to sit down first and count the cost, to see whether we can complete the tower, whether the army at our disposal (the "Our Father") is sufficient for the battle. It is impossible to take prayer lightly, for there is where we meet the radicalism of faith.

As long as we are not engaged in the combat of prayer, our radicalism is necessarily a discourse; and unfortunately, a discourse about God, or about humans, or about the absence of God, or about our society and has nothing radical in it. The radical begins where one takes God by force, where God is present. Radicalism is not *really* produced by some procedure of the intellect, or of the will to action, whatever it might be. It is brought about by the presence of God alone. The whole Bible, from beginning to end, attests that. It even constitutes, in all probability, the central theme of the kerygma.

Prayer is the precise point at which this radicalism is brought about in the unhindered meeting between God and humans. That is why it is a decisive combat and a final commitment. Such is the measure of the seriousness of the combat against God, to constrain God to become the One once again, in this age in which God has turned the other way.   —*PM*, 161–64

PRAYER AND SOCIAL PARTICIPATION

Total involvement in prayer demands of us a participation in society, in the lives of those close to us, of those at a distance, of intimate friends, and of strangers. Prayer has no limits. If it cannot be abstract it is (in contrast to agape) possible for large bodies of people, for those we do not know, precisely to the extent to which its substance and meaning come from God. But if prayer does not dispense from action, if it is the opposite to "rejection of the world," if it must relate constantly to events (and not lose itself in mystical, vague, and diffuse effusions), we still find it hard to believe today that prayer is more important than action.

It is indeed true that the content of prayer should be supplied by the world (in which our action is to be manifested), and that it is vain to pray abstractly. That is to say that normally our prayer should be generated by concrete situations, and that in the degree in which it is linked with action, it involves specific concern. It is useless to pray for peace or for justice, unless one is specific about what peace or what justice. Prayer must involve the courage of unilateral action, a courage of which the

Reformers gave proof when, after the example of the Psalmists and of Scripture, they did not hesitate to curse their enemies, according to Mottu.

Yet, however important this active viewpoint may be, it is prayer which dominates. With respect to the world, prayer is the act of bringing reality into the presence of God. We agree spontaneously to action, and then to add prayer to it, but the order is the reverse of that, namely, to pray, and then to act because of having prayed, as a function of that prayer. Of course, on behalf of action (on behalf of the practical), one can say that action alone is of any use. It is the only thing which does not lie. Its failures or successes are out in the open. It alone corresponds to human need today, hence to the second commandment. Finally, the present-day world is not made for contemplation. But in all that, we are faced, on the one hand, with the activist ideology, on the other hand, with a complete ignorance of the combat of prayer.

Prayer goes with action, but it is prayer which is radical and decisive. Every action will necessarily be taken over by the milieu in which it occurs. It will be turned aside from its purpose. It will be vitiated by circumstances. It will entail unforeseeable consequences and will drag misfortune in its train. Prayer, on the other hand, when it is genuine, cannot be taken over (since it obtains its import and substance from God). It attains its goal. It entails the consequences granted by God.

Action really receives its character from prayer. Prayer is what attests the finitude of action and frees it from its dramatic or tragic aspect. Since it shows that the action is not final, it brings to it humor and reserve. Otherwise we would be tempted to take it with dreadful seriousness. But in so doing prayer bestows upon action its greatest authenticity. It rescues action from activism, and it rescues the individual from bewilderment and despair in one's action. It prevents one from being engulfed in panic when one's action fails, and from being drawn into activism, when one is incited to more and more activity in pursuit of success, to the point of losing one's self. Prayer, because it is the warrant, the expression of my finitude, always teaches me that I must *be more* than my action; that I must live with my action, and even that my action must be lived with by another in *their* action. Thanks to prayer, I can see that truth about myself and my action, in hope and not in despair.

In this combat, the Christian who prays acts more effectively and more decisively on society than the person who is politically involved, with all the sincerity of one's faith put into the involvement. It is not a matter of seeing them in opposition to one another, but of inverting our instinctive, cultural hierarchy of values. The action is not the test of prayer, nor is it the proof of its importance or the measure of its genuineness. It is prayer which is the qualifying factor, the significance, the foundation of the truth of the action.

Apart from prayer, action is necessarily violence and falsehood. Even technological action, in spite of its appearance of neutrality and objectivity, is nevertheless in that category. Prayer is the only possible substitute for violence in human relations. Henceforth it is from prayer that one expects action to take its value. Action is no longer looked to for the immediate, visible, and expected result at any cost. Prayer guarantees the objective (perhaps unexpected) of action, but by that very fact, it cannot tolerate every action . . .

Thus prayer calls violence to account as a value, as an ultimate argument, as a means to be taken for granted. If we choose to use violence, so be it, but in that case let us stop playing the farce of prayer and love of neighbor. It is a decision one has to make. But we must be honest, and in so acting we should know (yet when we have chosen violence, we are no longer capable of knowing) that we are losing our best chance of success and our contact with truth. We should know, also, that our position is in the end far less radical, for in choosing violence we are participating completely in a world of violence, in a society in which violence reigns at every level and in all forms, in the ideology of the practical and of violence. As violent persons, we are fully conformed to the world. Violence is one of the "rudiments" (*stoicheia*) of this world.

Prayer, by contrast, is a much more radical break, a more fundamental protest. In that decision, in that combat, the world can have no part, since we have a share in the prayer, the sacrifice, and the resurrection of the one Jesus Christ. All further radicalism, of behavior, of style of life and of action, can only have the prior rupture of prayer as its source. Precisely because our technological society is given over entirely to action, the person who retires to one's room to pray is the true radical. Everything will flow from that. This act in society, which is also an action on this society, goes very much further than the concrete involvement, which it still does not shirk.

Prayer, in the degree in which it is the decision we have described, addressed to the One who issued the call in the first place, the Wholly Other and at the same time the Transcendent, is in reality the exact counterpoint of the rigorous mechanism of the technological society. It is the path which makes it possible to transform the individual's objectification and alienation. It is true independence with respect to the unfailing omnipotence of the state. It is a true nonconformity toward psychological ideologies and manipulations. It is all that in truth, in contrast to action which is called revolutionary, and which today is a pure illusion, a flight from the inexorable, a dream of a better day which is never to be. Prayer is flexibility within organizational rigidity. It is a positive challenge to the individualist–collectivist dilemma. Finally, it is the commitment which balances the fever for consumer goods and the obsession with efficacy. It is the sole necessary and sufficient action and practice, in a society which has lost its way.   —*PM*, 170–75

FAITH AND BELIEF

Two words call for notice, faith and belief. We have an annoying tendency to confuse the two. Belief is an everyday matter and sets the foundation for all that constitutes our existence. Everything depends on it; all human relations rest on it. Unless I have good reasons to the contrary, I believe spontaneously what people tell me: I have confidence in them a priori. If this were not so, human relations would be impossible, as in the kind of speech that only causes confusion or derision. I also believe scientific truths. I believe that E = mc2 because I have been told it. The whole educational system is based on belief. Students believe what their teachers or their books say; they learn on a basis of belief. We also believe spontaneously the witness of our senses, even when they are disturbed. We believe similarly in certain words, such as the good, or freedom, or justice, which we do not define plainly or consistently but to which we cling firmly no matter what their content. A society could not function if it did not rest on beliefs hidden in the deep recesses of each of its members and producing coherent sentiments and actions. A society without collective beliefs (which are, of course, individual in the eyes of each member) would soon fall into lawlessness and enter a process of dissolution. Beliefs are definitely the *raison d'être* of society.

Faith is very different—it is addressed to God. But beliefs may also be religious. There has always been an assimilation of belief to religion, and there still is. Religious beliefs are part of the whole. Often (in a debatable way) *religio* is connected with *religare*, "to tie." Religion binds people together and binds them as a group to their god. It is precisely this binding character that causes the problem, for it plunges us into a sociological analysis of religion. It is finally for the sake of fellowship with one another that people refer to a more lofty being or god that will serve as a group guarantee and symbol. The objects of this religion may be very different, whether one or more gods

projected in heaven, or the Universal. Other dimensions than the
human can be apotheosized. Reason can be deified, or science.
Hitlerism made its own religion, as did Marxism–Leninism up
to the 1970s. The country can be regarded as divine. Progress
has become a key term in modern religion. Each cult has its own
rites and myths and heretics and believers and *raison d'être* and
believing potential. But the object of religion is not necessarily
God.

Faith in God—in a God who does not incarnate some natural force or who is not the abstract and hypostatized projection
of one of our own desires or aspirations or values (Feuerbach),
faith in a God who is different from all that we can conceive or
imagine—cannot be assimilated to belief. For this God cannot
be assimilated to one of the representations that we might easily multiply. If God is God, God is inevitably different from all
that polytheists call god. Each of those gods can be described
and defined; each has its own function and sphere of action.
But the God of faith is inaccessible and inassimilable. God is so
fundamentally other (if God were not, if God could be measured
against one of our values or beliefs, God would not be God) that
we can neither define nor contemplate God. The God of faith is
totally inaccessible. The affirmation of Feuerbach, that God is an
absolutized value, was simplistic and puerile. For one thing, we
have no idea of what the absolute or the infinite is. We cannot
say anything about it or assimilate it. To talk about an absolutized value might be to talk about God, but it is not possible for
human beings to absolutize anything.

In regard to the innumerable attacks made upon God, we may
simply say that those who make them do not know what they
are talking about. Often with just cause they are attacking the
image of God that in a given time and place people have made.
But this is their own image of God, made for convenience—it is
not God. A commonly repeated formula that is now accepted as
self-evident is that we have made God in our own image. But to

say this is not to know what one is saying; it is childish prattle. For if God is God, then all that we can say about God is just our own approximation or perception, as when a child takes a pail of seawater, stirs it until it foams, and then says he is carrying the ocean and its waves. On our own we know nothing about God. Only when God chooses to reveal a tiny part of God's being do we achieve a tiny knowledge and recognition.

In this revelation God has to put Godself on our level of apprehension, on our cultural and intellectual level, if what God wants to communicate is to be accessible. Thus there are variations, not because God is variable, but because those whom God addresses are. God uses the most appropriate means to establish communication with us—the word. When God addresses Godself to a person, it is always a very personal interrelation . . .

We can see now the difference between faith in God and all beliefs. A belief that enables society to maintain itself is necessarily collective. Apt at seizing on the fullness of its object, it is an uplifting force that carries us above ourselves (even though it may do much mischief when it pretends to be absolute and exclusive). Faith is at every point the opposite. First of all it is a personal relation. It does not grasp the fullness of him to whom it is directed. It is not useful to society; on the contrary, it is a disturbing force, causing breaks in social ties. Above all, it can arise only because it is God who comes down to us. This is the key point. Belief always tries to mount up to what it regards as God. Faith receives God who comes down from his transcendence to set himself on the level of the child that he wishes to rejoin. No two things could be more different.   —*WIB*, 2–5

FAITH AS INTERPLAY

Faith is constant interplay; it never stagnates or settles down. One can never be "all love" or "holy" in and of oneself, nor can one incarnate faith in some static, definitive fashion. In its attempts to live out this love faith is the perennially new critical

point. Thus faith necessarily moves right ahead to criticize itself.
It constantly measures the distance separating the faith of Jesus
and of Abraham from the faith I myself am living. It disconnects
me more and more from myself, from the encroachments of my
self-critical ego. It keeps a watchful eye out for whatever might
imprison it in arrogant solitude (proud of its own righteousness
and unrelenting conviction), as well as for whatever might transform it into belief. Faith therefore implies the continual presence
of temptation and an ever clearer vision of reality; it implies
criticism of Christian religion, of civilizing missions, of Christian moral codes imposed from the outside, of a Christian truth
that excludes claims to it from any other area of human culture.
The first task of faith in Christ is inevitably to criticize all of
faith's "constructive" extensions in politics and morality, which
are inevitable but nothing more than so many forms of betrayal.

The model we should always keep in mind is Kierkegaard, a
man whose faith really did reach a critical mass. And let's not
have any silly talk about masochism. What I'm referring to is
what traditional biblical language calls repentance, but the idea
has been cheapened, coarsened, hackneyed, and softened into a
kind of *moral* regret. But there's nothing of that in revelation.
The Word of God holds out a mirror to me in which I see myself
as I am, where I discover simultaneously how impossible it is
for me to believe that word and how impossible it is to break
away from it. Again, this has nothing to do with masochism:
from one end to the other the Bible keeps telling us that God's
judgment *begins* with the judgment of his faithful. The Old Testament announces that judgment begins with Israel (as we have
seen, alas, over and over again). In the New Testament judgment
begins with the church, which is the first to be weighed in the
scales. This, and nothing more or less, is what faith as the critic
of faith means in the concrete reality of our day-to-day lives.

But this can't be separated from its other aspect, faith as the
point of rupture (not with our fellow human beings) but with

religions. Starting from there, faith *must* proceed to criticize, to judge (in this case, yes), and radically to reject all human religious claims. We have to be careful here: it's not people who are being judged or criticized here; it's their will to power and the expression of that in religion. Faith does not reject human speech, quite the contrary. Faith is always listening, always on the alert, always attentive to people's words, to their fears, their hopes, their passions, and their hymns. It never judges anything against the norm of an abstract, frozen morality. It has its ears open to questions, knowing that it can't answer them intellectually. Instead it puts us at the heart of the same questions, the same dramas, the same impossibilities. The only answer we have to give is ourselves, such as we are, while pointing to the one who transposes our questions into others that we can, in fact, answer, because we have been made answer-able by love.

—*LF*, 180–81

FAITH AND FREEDOM

I would hope that readers have grasped my meaning: in all that I have said there is no room for solutions or "usefulness." And as for solving on our own the problems we're tangled in—we don't have a chance in the world.

My thesis is that either there exists a "truth-reality" that cannot be assimilated by the forces unleashed in our time—and if so we have a possible future—or else it does not exist, and then we might as well resign ourselves because human history is finished. As of now. In this context faith is our responsibility to see to it that the Transcendent, the Unconditioned, the Totally Other Being, becomes an active reality here and now, because it's not simply God's existence all by itself that gives us the answer. And we must not count on his waving the magic wand to change our situation. Faith moves mountains only when it speaks to the omnipotent Creator, and when it also accepts its role of hearing the word of faith. But this faith must bring us to decide on our own course of action, which will find its source, its *raison d'*être in the unassimilable and unknowable Truth, which becomes by way of faith the reality that sets us free.   —*LF*, 196–97

LOVE OF OTHERS

But I love people as they are. I love them in this evil, this perversion, this cruelty. I love individuals. I love them because in all the evil that they do they are essentially unhappy and not just malefactors. I do not say that they can be excused. The evil they do is still evil. I do not advocate irresponsibility. That would be to dishonor them. No, they are responsible. But they are also unhappy, and I consider this first rather than their wickedness or their imbecility. There are no degrees. All are guilty. But all are also unhappy, even the executioners of Auschwitz and Pol Pot. As the poet puts it, it is no exaggeration when people say that they are naked and that they tremble, that they are unhappy, that they are under the stroke of death and cold, when they say that they shiver and tremble, that they are wanderers with no refuge, that they are under the stroke of man and God. I have devoted my whole life to making people more aware, more free, more capable of judging themselves, of getting out of the crowd, of choosing, and at the same time of avoiding wickedness and imbecility. My books have never had any other goal. Of all the people that I have met, no matter what they are, I can say that I have tried to love them. I have lived my whole life in terms of the great theological affirmation: "God so loved the world [the place of absolute evil] that he gave his only Son, that whoever believes in him should be saved and have eternal life" (John 3:16).

Human beings are the most surprising beings imaginable, for the very people who are so evil have a fundamental thirst for good. They do evil but they aspire after good. They want a world of justice and liberty. They are moved by the sight of the misery of starving people. Even when they do ill to others, they always try to justify themselves. For a long time I thought that such attempted justification merely redoubled the evil. I said that I would accept what people did so long as they did not look for excuses to show that they had good reason to do it. Undoubtedly there is truth in this view. I still believe that excuses add hypocrisy to the evil. At the same time, however, the attempt at self-justification is an expression of the thirst for good. We cannot be content to do an evil that is simply an evil and is recognized as such. We have to give ourselves a certificate of good conduct. In other words we can never be purely and simply cynical. When we come before the just Judge, we cannot look him in the face and simply say: "All right, I did it, and that is all there is to it." We always act as Adam did when first he fled and then he blamed someone else (his wife), or as Cain did. We have to convince ourselves that we have done good even when we have done evil. We are pursuing such goods as liberty, happiness, equality, progress, country, truth, or love. Millions of our neighbors are killed in the pursuit of such goods. Convinced that there is good in what we have done, we have no remorse precisely because of this thirst for good. We kill to save. Think of the unheard-of action of the church when it burned heretics and witches, not to punish them, but to save their souls. Such an act was called an *auto-da-fé*, an act of faith. I am not accusing anyone of hypocrisy. I believe that this thirst for good is one of the deepest of human tendencies even though we can only do evil, and if we could only be aware of what we are doing we would agree at once with the statement of Paul: "Wretched man that I am! I do not do the good I want, and I do the evil that I hate" (see Romans 7:15, 25). The essential difference is that Paul, thanks to the light of the Holy Spirit, clearly perceives and takes note of his situation, whereas those outside the Christian faith glory in doing evil, convinced that it is for a greater good.

—*WIB*, 64–65

3

Myths, Idols, and the Demonic

Jacques Ellul wrote that the three most pernicious elements of modern industrial society are technique, money, and power. The term technique *refers simultaneously to the proliferation of technology and—even more fundamentally—a worldview that mirrors the values of technology: an overly calculative mind-set governed by a drive for efficiency. Unfortunately, technique is often translated into English simply as* technology, *which has led to some distortion of its meaning.*

The myths of unending technological and scientific progress have profoundly aided technique in its unfettered growth, leading to what Ellul called a pantechnocracy. *They have also caused widespread exploitation, alienation, and ecological destruction. Inseparable from technique is money: both a myth and an idol. Ellul sought to awaken his readers to see that we are owned and controlled by our money: slaves to its dictates and limits. The notion that more money leads to more freedom is a downright lie, says Ellul. Closely intertwined with technique and money is politics, which Ellul described as the* realm of the demonic. *While technique and money are contributing factors, it is the modern political apparatus that directly causes violence and coerces us to accept competition and power as the norm.*

TECHNOLOGICAL TOTALITARIANISM

The more is known about human nature, the more people insist on the importance of creative disorder and at the same time the more humanity becomes assimilated to a highly regulated order. Similarly the more humane bureaucracies become, the more they become, in reality, rigorous and absolute. And all this culminates in pantechnocracy, which leaves no earthly domain unplundered. There is no foreseeable limit to the spread of technology that has entered on the path of complete ingestion of natural resources, of nature itself, of human beings, and everything in existence. The process of technological growth is intrinsically totalitarian. Nothing can stop it except the actual disappearance of the fuel it feeds on: raw materials, space, objects of every kind, and ultimately human beings. All the nuances and fine distinctions are useless here. Technology can't come to a halt until it has reached the barrier of absolute finitude, when *everything* has been technologized.

That means that these manifold powers combine to form an ensemble that is doubtless incoherent but even so constitutes a totality that has never existed before, other than as our galaxy. This is, in effect, the disappearance of the human being as an individual and a person, and the emergence of the human as fragment, as cell, cog, switch, coded number, of the human as an opportunity, a bacterium, a pretext, a microprocessor of the unified ensemble that absorbs all things into its unanimous disorder. The only hope, given this situation, lies in a reality utterly beyond the reach of that limitless expansion, that is, located beyond finitude, outside the realities accessible to technology, in an essentially inaccessible reality. That is to say, God.

—*LF*, 194–95

TECHNOLOGICAL MORALITY

A transformation in the lived morality is taking place under our own eyes. We are entering into a new form of morality which could be called technological morality, since it tends to bring human behavior into harmony with the technological world, to set up a new scale of values in terms of technology, and to create new virtues . . .

Technology supposes the creation of a new morality. It informs the whole of public, professional, and private life. One can no longer act except in relation to technical ensembles. Hence there is need to create new patterns of behavior, new ideas, new virtues. At the same time, new choices are set before humans which they are in no way prepared to face. Now the more technology is precise, exacting, and efficient, the more it demands that the performer be efficient, precise, prepared. These are not merely questions of competence. They are matters requiring dedication. This modern person must know how to use the technique, but must also know how to be its servant. One's moral qualities must be at the level of the new world which technology is unveiling . . .

Technological morality exhibits two principal characteristics. It is above all a morality of behavior and second, it excludes moral questioning. It is a morality of behavior. That is to say, it is solely interested in the human's external conduct. The problems of intention, sentiment, ideals, perplexities of conscience, are none of its concern. Still, it ignores these only as long as they remain inward. If these interior movements were to lay claim to outward expression, then the technological morality would enter into conflict with them, for conduct must always be determined by external and objective motives if human attitudes are to be consistent with the technological world in which one must live and act. The situation calls for a behavior on the part of humans which is exact, precise, in harmony with the working of all the categories of techniques which are proliferating in our society. And this behavior should be fixed, not on the basis of moral principles, but in terms of precise technological rules—psychological and sociological. The external act alone has value, and this act should be determined for technological motives. This is one of the principal results of the sciences, which—in spite of their proclamations and declarations—are all and always sciences impregnated with morality aimed at adapting humans to the technological world . . .

In this technological morality there is also set up a scale of values which are truly valid for humans and which the individual accepts as such. Without doubt, one of the important facts in this sphere is the transformation of technology itself into a value. For the individual of today technology is not only a fact. It is not merely an instrument, a means. It is a criterion of good and evil. It gives meaning to life. It brings promise. It is a reason for acting and it demands our commitment . . . But this is even more exact at the level of the average person. Doubtless, for this person, in various ways, technology is a value. In various ways, because the meaning which technology has given to the average person's life can as well be comfort, the possession of an appliance, rather than the liberation of the proletariat thanks to technology, or humanity's newfound happiness. This is a criterion of good and evil, for without the slightest doubt everyone today treats technology as a good (a gift of God, etc.), and people cannot avoid talking that way . . .

But we must pass on to a second value of this technological morality, that of the normal. In this technological society the normal tends to replace the moral. One is no longer asked to act well, but to act normally. The norm is no longer an imperative of the conscience. One gets at it through average behavior, whether this is determined statistically, or by psychological evaluation, or by whatever means. Everything concurs in confirming the predominance of the normal. Increasingly the criminal is treated as a sick, abnormal person, in need of care to help him return to average, normal behavior. Similarly, the highest virtue demanded of one today is adjustment. The worst judgment one can suffer is to be called maladjusted. (Maladjusted to what? Very exactly, to the technological society. Sociologists and psychologists are

agreed in acknowledging that technology is the most frequent
cause of maladjustment.) The chief purpose of instruction and
education today is to bring along a younger generation which is
adjusted to this society . . .

Finally, we should bear in mind a third value characteristic of
this morality; namely, success. In the last analysis, good and evil
are synonyms for success and failure. According to the bourgeois
formula, stemming from a particular interpretation of the Bible,
virtue is always ratified by material success. But with the passage
of time (and the temptation was too great for this to be avoided)
the conclusion was drawn that success is the clear sign of virtue,
since it is virtue's reward. Virtue is invisible. Success is visible.
Hence success allows us to presuppose the existence of virtue.
The next step is to say that success is, in itself, the good. One
is an abbreviation for the other. With this orientation one then
seeks to base morality on success, whence the demonstration
that "crime doesn't pay." When all is said and done, the reason
one should not be a criminal is that it isn't profitable. But if we
proceed in this direction we are obliged to admit that strength
is one of the essential factors of success, and then we very soon
realize that the crucial polarity is not so much that of good and
evil as that of strength and weakness—thence, also, the ethical
importance of the champion.

—*TWTD*, 185, 187–88, 190, 192–93

DESACRALIZED HISTORY AND SCIENCE

Today we could say that the two fundamental myths of modern humans are history and science. There is no need to go into
a lengthy analysis of their origin and characteristics. That has
been done many times. Let us simply consider that they are the
bases for all the beliefs, ideologies, actions, and feelings of the
twentieth-century individual. History has been transmuted into
a value, which makes it the judge of good and evil . . .

We are here in the presence of a significant mutation. It is known that history traditionally had a sacred meaning. It wasn't a matter of describing events, but of gaining from them an exemplary, meaningful account. History was one of the instruments of myth. Traditionally it had no value except in its integration into a myth. Now we have changed all that. We have secularized history. It now consists in a recounting of events without reference to the eternal, and in a tracing of their unfolding without looking for a meaning. It is desacralized.

But, by an amazing turnabout, at the very moment of the desacralization of history, we see constituted the myth of history. No longer is history integrated into a myth. No longer does it serve a sacred. It *is* the meaning, in and of itself. It is no longer referred to the eternal, because it contains within itself the value of the eternal. Perhaps one of the most remarkable general phenomena of our time is that by which the desacralized universe becomes sacred through the very fact of being desacralized . . .

But more than that, there is the problem of meaning. We have said that history of itself has become significant, and that has two sides: it is endowed with meaning and it gives meaning. The second depends on the first. The major problem stems from the fact that history no longer receives meaning from something outside of history: God, truth, freedom, etc. History itself is all-inclusive. Nothing any longer is extra-historical (and that indeed is mythical). Hence it has to get its meaning from itself. The meaning cannot be obtained from a philosophy of history, which would again have an external reference. It can come only from the very structure of history itself.

If history has a structure, then it has a meaning. That is what made dialectical materialism a success. The dialectical movement of history guarantees the meaning. Through it we have the key to humankind, to human past and future, and everything gets its value from that dialectic. There is no need to look elsewhere, because elsewhere, by definition, is not subject to this dialectic, and consequently it could have nothing to do with history. It could not even exist, since it is impossible to conceive of anything existing not subject to history. Conversely, if from its very structure history has an intrinsic meaning, then since everything is inserted into history, everything receives meaning through that insertion—each life, each decision takes on value and truth because it shares in the meaning of history.

This basic myth, this general line which underlies all modern myths, also displays the completely mythical quality of being valid for all degrees of awareness, irrespective of social categories. The philosopher and the journalist, the average person and the member of the proletariat, young and old, white and black, fascist and leftist, everybody and at all levels of intelligence and interpretation, submit without hesitation to this implicit verity, which is both diffuse and conscious, and which has become the *ultima ratio* of the wisdom of our time. How could we refuse to qualify it as a myth?

The second fundamental myth is science. We find the same constituent factors as in the preceding case. On the one hand, there is the transition from a sacred science to a desacralized/ desacralizing science. There was science as the preserve of the magi and the cabalists, the secret-sacred whose remains are observed by modern research into the secrets of the Great Pyramid or the Inca civilization. Then is brought to light a method of comprehending and apprehending the real which implies that the real is no longer sacred, and that the method can no longer be secret. From being esoteric, science became exoteric. It was constituted within itself, without reference to the outside, and everything it examined became desacralized.

Following upon this, there came into being a discourse about science, and that is the second aspect. One witnessed an increasing gap between what scientists were doing in their laboratories, the patient research, the cautious conclusions, the abandonment of explanations, the refusal to generalize, the challenging of causalities, mathematical abstraction as a representation and a method—and, on the other hand, the grandiose, grandiloquent discourse about science, such as was heard at the time of Sputnik, or of the first landing on the moon . . .

This belief in the universal capacity of science is now associated with the faith that science is the destiny of humankind. One lives (and cannot live otherwise) in the scientific cosmos. Science discloses one's origin, justifies one's present, and assures one's future. Of course the scientist's science does none of that, and doesn't pretend to. But it has such prestige and produces such magnificent results, it stands for such great value, that, in generalized global discourse, this can be brought out only in the form of myth. Science is thought of as undertaking everything, in conjunction with history. We expect everything of science, as of an awe-inspiring and benevolent divinity, which plays a central and mysterious, yet well-known role in the story which modern humanity is telling itself . . .

To the degree, in fact, to which objectivity stems from pure methodology, then becomes a state of consciousness, an attitude, an ethic, it becomes a value judgment, an exclusion of every other mode of apprehending truth. That relation to truth introduces us into the mythical.   —*ND*, 98–99, 101–2

HAPPINESS AND PROGRESS

The "belief-image" of happiness is likewise founded on science. The recipes for happiness hitherto proposed to humans were based on individual experience, on an exercise of the reason or of the body, and almost always, even in the case of Epicurus, on a discipline. What is now being substituted is a collective, materialistic possibility, namely, a happiness guaranteed through scientific progress.

All have a right to it. All are actually promised it. There is no need for any sacrifice, any education, any decision, and any responsibility. Happiness is due everybody, and it consists in a growth in collective riches, for this happiness is purely material. Thus what was only a vague dream for the masses and difficult research for intellectuals has completely altered its character in our society. It is a precise image, capable of realization and shared by all.

The myth of happiness is what makes it possible for modern humans to feel that life is worth living. Without that promised happiness, why live? Justice, truth, virtue—all fade into the darkness of vanity before the triumphant conviction that the realization of happiness is the one thing to be taken seriously. All activity should be given over to that exclusive end, and it is impossible to conceive of life and the future except under the auspices of happiness.

Here, again, we note that the myth is gloriously shared by all, and connected by all to scientific development. The sole difference between communists and the bourgeoisie is a disagreement over what means are best suited to furnish people with this plenitude of happiness. The power of the myth is enough to legitimize without hesitation all crimes and all sacrifices. The elimination of the bourgeoisie is all that is needed for the totality of the people to achieve happiness. The Nazi officers entering France in 1940 could say, "We are coming to bring you happiness."

Every expression of doubt about this myth, however slight, is enough to cause the doubter to be looked upon as an enemy of humanity. Do you doubt that American civilization, in its orientation toward the achievement of happiness, is justified by that alone? You are "un-American." Do you doubt that the number one problem of the world is hunger? Do you think that the happiness of eating, extended to the masses in India or South America, could be paid for by a higher price than life is worth? You are an enemy of humanity. If you talk like that, you are a bourgeois with a full stomach. This is an assumption of myth which makes it possible to classify as wicked all who do not share it.

That brings us to one of the major mythical aspects of our time: the "power-image" of progress. This is located at the pivotal point of the two fundamental beliefs—science and history—and it shares as much in the one as in the other. Science cannot but lead us from progress to progress. That myth was born with the explosion of marvels before the bedazzled eyes of nineteenth-century humans. Then there is history, which unveils for us the slow, secret, mysterious advance of humankind, driven, from origins onward, toward a fulfillment better and better implemented, better and better understood, albeit through hesitations and even retrogressions.

It is a movement of freedom and democracy, from the beginnings of history to its flowering in the nineteenth century. It is a movement of reason, triumphing over the darkness in science itself, as hailed by Auguste Comte. It is a movement of work, which now has reached its point of triumph and its hour of truth in the ceaseless struggle against the exploiter. Those are three examples of one and the same belief in progress, bearing simply on different symbols . . .

If we are so well equipped in reason and faith, the question has to be asked whether it is at all possible not to share in the belief. This apparently irreversible movement, this characterization of history at our own level—can we refuse to grasp it and to be grasped by it? Such a thing is even less possible as the movement itself is more rapid. No longer is human progress seen over millennia, but in the course of a single lifetime. How could I escape taking up a position for or against?—and how be against, since progress is inevitable?

But myth is also characterized by its extrapolation from what is to what ought to be. The progress we see as being so unmistakable is the progress of machines, of technology, of material means as a whole. The progress of institutions is less certain, and the progress within humankind is probably nonexistent. Neither intelligence nor virtue seems very superior now to what it was four or five thousand years ago. The best we might be able to say is that we know nothing about it.

Now it is precisely the individual in the grip of the myth of progress who does know about it. One knows with a certainty that human progress goes along with progress in things, and that one's inventions are proof of one's greater intelligence and truth. Indeed it has to be that way, for otherwise the whole thing might turn into a catastrophe. There isn't the slightest doubt in anyone's mind that people today are better, more intelligent, and more suited for self-government than the Athenian of the fifth century. If we project this toward the future, we have the same certitude that the human of tomorrow will have all it takes to resolve the problems we are unable to overcome.

Thus, not only does progress exist, it is also undeniably good. It has improved the human lot and is headed in the direction of the good. What lunacy, therefore, to think to pass judgment on it, or to oppose it! What lunacy and what evil! Myth always makes it possible for the person possessed by it to judge from the height of one's certitudes any outside observer. Anyone today who has questions on the subject of progress is the butt of the most bitter and contemptuous judgment, a judgment brought unanimously by those of the right and of the left.

—ND, 105–7

POLITICS AS THE REALM OF THE DEMONIC

Politics is the acquisition of power: the means necessary for getting it, and once you get it the means for defending yourself against the enemy and so holding on to it. But what does one use it for—for goodness and virtue? No, one uses it for power; it's an end in itself. And that's all there is to politics. All the fine talk about politics as a means of establishing justice, so forth and so forth, is nothing but a smokescreen that on the one hand conceals harsh, vulgar reality and on the other justifies the universal passion for politics, the universal conviction that everything is political, that politics is the most noble human activity, whereas it is really the most ignoble. It is, strictly speaking, the source of all the evils that plague our time. And when I say that it is diabolical and satanic, I mean these adjectives literally.

Politics is diabolical. The devil can be the one who *divides*, separates, disjoins, disrupts communions, brings about divorce, and breaks up dialogue. In the Bible the devil is the one who instigates the break between God and humankind, who uses various means to shatter the communion that once linked the creator with creation. He takes advantage of perfectly natural and healthy human instincts: God creates humans free, bidding them govern creation and subdue it. The devil induces them to declare themselves independent of God's will, to seek autonomy. And in the same way he transforms the power given by God into a will to dominate.

This kind of distortion is typical of the way the devil acts, pretending to accomplish God's work, while transforming it into its opposite. And this is also where idealistic politics—the highly moral, community-oriented sort—turns into the real politics I mentioned before. To achieve this reversal, the Bible says that the devil operates through seduction (Eve looks at the "tree" and plainly sees that it is beautiful, good, pleasing, intelligent, etc.) and through what is often called lies (the devil is the father of lies), but what is rather exploitation of truth to produce effects contrary to those of the truth. Thus in the dialogue between Eve and the devil, the latter doesn't lie. He does inform her that people will be as gods, determining good and evil, and that they will not die. But basically he seduces by shifting meanings and values. Finite reality becomes ultimate truth. And finite reality puts people in a situation different from the one they had imagined or hoped for as they peered through the glimmerings and refractions of the devil's seductive speech.

Now speaking concretely of society today, what is the father of lies? It is politics, and I would go so far as to say politics alone. France is divided into two blocs, which fact is absurd enough, because we know very well that both are largely interchangeable, that it's six of one, half a dozen of the other. But France is divided nonetheless. There are the victors and the vanquished, labeled as such by politics—and the terms are nothing but labels. There is White imperialism and Red imperialism, ready to go to war against each other. And what is it that drives nations straight to war, even though in general and on their own they have no such thought in mind? Politics.

What makes boys from Texas go off and kill Vietnamese, and boys from Estonia go off and kill Afghans? Only politics, which claims to represent the common good, collective interests, the homeland, and all that. Obviously, there are groups and clans who don't agree with each other, tribes, families, and corporations that are hostile to one another. But this doesn't have any terrible consequences—it leads at most to vendettas. But when these local interests are taken in hand by politics, then they come to stand for the general good. And then we find ourselves in collective tragedies where the innocent pay for the guilty.

When this happens, it's useless to talk about economic interests being more fundamental: without political structures, strategies, installations, and ideologies, economic interests are nothing and can do little to change conditions. It is politics that conquers colonies and markets (with a good deal, admittedly, of economic profit), politics that mobilizes people for wars that economic interests have made inevitable. And even if it isn't always true that politics is motivated by economics, still politics is the divisive force par excellence. It is politics and not economics that causes class divisions and shapes class struggle.

—LF, 235–37

DELIBERATE AMNESIA

We have just spoken of the inability to foresee the future (which is a danger only because we are unleashing unsuspected forces).

But at the same time we are witnessing the disappearance of the past, the widespread loss of both collective and individual memory. A few years ago an important book was published with the title *Hitler? Never Heard of Him*. People in our society are creatures without memory; step by step they forget everything. This means that they have no past and no roots. And so these people—us—have no foreseeable future and no past to build on, neither familial, nor local, nor communal, nor national, nothing at all.

How, then, could you expect them not to be afraid, these people from no-place, who don't know where they're coming from or going to? And when they become afraid, how could they not get violent? Only the fearful are violent, as we know in the case of dogs. It's the same with people.

Forgetfulness or amnesia is one of the striking features of today's psychological landscape, spontaneous forgetfulness, erasing a past without glory, adventure, or satisfaction. Sometimes this oblivion is an unconscious blotting out of remorse, of our own perverse acts—and we have been well schooled in the necessity of getting rid of guilt feelings. But there is also a free and deliberate forgetfulness in the face of powers aiming to obliterate our history at any cost. No, this is not 1984. But it *is* a reign of amnesia in all quarters, all classes, and all governments. The past is rejected, and everything is staked on the future. People rush headlong to prepare themselves for the twenty-first century. It all makes one think of a rudderless boat cut adrift and swept along with the current.

The mad passion for progress stays with us, though we can already taste the bitterness of its fruits. Onward, ever onward, tomorrow will surely realize the dream of . . . And so each one of us carefully buries in oblivion the self we were yesterday. I shall not go into what I consider the outrageously facile denials and contradictory affirmations of which Sartre was the master, the model, the guru, but which one now hears from almost all intellectuals, scientists, politicians, and the militant followers of

various movements. They have long since left behind the stage
where they clearly realized, and had qualms of conscience over
the fact, that they were in the process of worshiping what they
had condemned the day before and of condemning what they
once worshiped.

You meet fervent communists, once Stalinists, who brazenly
tell you, "But of course, everybody knows Stalin was a blood-
thirsty tyrant, and anyhow he never represented real communism." Or you meet anti-Christians who have had a sudden
illumination (of what?) and converted. But unlike Paul or
Augustine (no road to Damascus here), they never recall either
their life of debauchery or their violent resistance to Christianity.
Oh no, that never existed. Conversion is the great miracle. God
exists; they have laid hands on him. Before this? There was no
"before"; it didn't exist. Simple as that . . .

We have become totally irresponsible in the political and economic positions we take; we have forgotten ourselves and our
fellow citizens. As I said twenty years ago, one piece of information dislodges another. There is no continuity, no coherence. We
live in a culture of forgetfulness, a culture that suits us very well,
enabling us to be blown about by every gust of wind, while we
gravely affirm the stability of our opinions. This is a culture that
also suits our governments, because a people without memory is
infinitely easier to manipulate. History is being eliminated from
the schools for the same reason. All education is being reduced
to the indispensable prerequisites for "taking part in the society of tomorrow"—a grotesque proposition since nobody in the
world knows what that society will be . . .

The most important kind of forgetfulness is political. Our
recent experience of this runs deep, as we have seen how literally everything can be forgotten, by writers, by the public, even
by the opposition party. How prophetic were Nietzsche's words
in *Beyond Good and Evil*, "Blessed are the forgetful, for they
shall recover even from their own stupid mistakes." That is most
certainly true, but people who live submerged in forgetfulness

cannot help being beset by fears about the present, which seem incomparable, unheard of, insurmountable, because they have lost all their memories of war, famine, errors, obstacles, lies, wandering in the desert, persecution, all the things that past generations in their obstinate will to live managed to overcome.

But we don't overcome anymore, the art has been lost, and people are afraid of everything. They are like a body no longer capable of immunizing itself because it has lost the "memory" of previous diseases. Our society as a whole has become incapable of producing the antibodies needed to triumph over adversity, because their source could only be, not programs, plans, or doctrines, but vital social and political experience. They could arise only from memory, from the flesh and spirit of everything we have lived through, from all the lessons painfully learned, all the meanings laboriously built on those human experiences.

—*LF*, 225–28

AWARENESS

The first duty of a Christian . . . is the duty of awareness: that is to say, the duty of understanding the world and oneself, inseparably connected and inseparably condemned, in their reality. This means the refusal to accept appearances at their face value, and of information for information's sake, the refusal of the abstract phenomenon, the refusal of the illusion given by present means, the consoling illusion of "progress," and of the improvement of situations and of humans, by a sort of benevolent fatalism of history.

The first act, the first necessity, for this awareness, is a fierce and passionate destruction of myths, of intellectual outmoded doctrines . . . it is the shattering of this intellectual bourgeois outlook which is "conformism" in thought, whether to a dogma (as in Russia), or to a way of life (as in the United States); it is the violent break with this pageant of information and of "news," and the deflation, by a strict exegesis, of interpretations and "balloons" which people try to present to us as capable of elevating the world. But in the name of what is this offer made?

The second element in awareness is the will to find objective reality, to discover the facts of the life led by the people who surround me. This is the creation of genuine realism, such as I tried to describe in my work on political realism already quoted: but here, again, we are obliged to ask the question: "In the name of what?"

The third element consists in the fact that this reality ought to be grasped first of all on the human level. We must refuse energetically to be detached from this sphere, a level which is not very high, but is the only significant one. This means that first of all we must get rid of evasion, in all its forms, in the ideal, in the future, in abstraction. We must no longer think of "humankind" in the abstract, but of my neighbor Mario. It is in the concrete life of this man, which I can easily know, that I see the real repercussions of the machine, of the press, of political discourses and of the administration. If people say: "It all depends on whether we are looking at a farmer in Texas, or a farmer in the Soviet Union"—I don't know anything about this (and I won't learn that from newspaper reports), but I think I am right, because I believe in human nature.

I refuse to believe in the "progress" of humanity, when I see from year to year the lowering of standards among men I know, whose lives I follow, in the midst of whom I live—when I see how they lose their sense of responsibility, their seriousness in work, their recognition of a true authority, their desire for a decent life—when I see them weighed down by anxiety about what the great ones of the earth are plotting, by the fear which penetrates our world, by the hatred which they feel for a terrible phantom which they cannot even name; when I see them cornered by circumstances, and, as they suffer, becoming thieves and frauds, embittered, avaricious, selfish, unbelieving, full of resistance and rancor, or when I see them engaged in a desperate

struggle, which comes from the depths of their being, against
something they do not know . . .

The fourth element in this awareness consists in looking at
present problems as profoundly as possible, to see them as they
are, with, on the one hand, the implacable ways of our world,
and, on the other hand, the situation in which we, as humans,
are placed. It is for us to find, behind the facts presented to us,
the reality on which they are based; thus behind the various
aspects of propaganda, this reality, common to all countries and
all states, which is propaganda itself, apart from its sentimental
or ideological content, without any real importance. We have to
find, behind the theories which splash us and blind us from every
quarter, the reality which they hide from us. For instance, behind
the democratic or totalitarian aspects, the reality of the life of the
technician, which goes its own way, whatever the setting may be.
What we need is to find the true structure or framework of our
modern civilization, though in order to get down to this we may
have to do a great deal of difficult and delicate scraping away of
extraneous matter. We need to understand this framework as the
expression of the spiritual reality of our civilization, our present
expression of the spiritual reality of the world . . .

Once more, in whose name are we to do and say such things?
Thanks to what can we achieve this upheaval which seems
impossible? At bottom, what this "awareness" means, is the
rediscovery in every sphere of life of the reality which all the
world is seeking. And what shall we do by ourselves in this argument? How are we to come to know this spiritual reality which
conditions material reality? (We see it, indeed, in experience, but
we cannot go any further.)

In short, to achieve this awareness as a whole is only possible
under the illumination of the Holy Spirit. Here we are pulled up
sharply—we can go no further. We can see what is necessary, and
many people have been able, until now, to agree about this, but
we have not found either the means or the reason, that is, the

motive force to achieve it . . . In other words, today neither intellectual effort nor activity can possibly bring us to this awareness of the world in which we live. Now it is necessary to have an exterior intervention because our civilization is absolutely totalitarian, and we cannot extricate ourselves from it. But there is no longer any exterior force in the world. Our society absorbs all forms of intelligence. Thus, because our civilization is more than human, we must perceive that it is not made by "flesh and blood" but by the "principalities . . . and . . . powers . . . the world-rulers of this darkness . . ." But nothing in our intellectual training prepares us either to see or to understand this. Our intellectual methods are purely materialistic, and entirely inadequate for such profound awareness to become possible. It is, indeed, true that it is only the intervention of the Holy Spirit which can transform our intelligence, in such a way that it will not be swallowed up by our systems, and that it will be sufficiently penetrating. Today no other possibility exists.

—*PK*, 119–20, 121, 123–24

THE MODERN SACRED AND ICONOCLASM

Surely the confrontation at the present time between Christianity and our western technological society is very valuable and instructive. It is true that Christianity, mongrelized since the seventeenth century, has been in need of a sort of cultural revolution . . . It is possible that Christianity may be passing through fire from which it should emerge purified, but that is not at all certain . . .

When God enters the picture, God destroys the human's sacred. It is true that God secularizes (and, to be sure, that God opens the door to human action on a secularized nature), but one forgets that it is the word of God which secularizes, and not philosophy, science, or technology—that this word of God is independent of our analyses, and that either it is given in the Bible and in the incarnation or it is just our imagination. It is forgotten that in this word of God there is attestation of human sin, of the rupture between humans and God, of the human's situation within evil. To void that, to reduce it is, on the one hand, to render the remainder of the revelation completely meaningless, and on the other hand, it is to prevent oneself any longer from seeing modern human's sacralizing, for this human creates a sacred for one's self and finds a religion only in order to counter the prior situation. To deny that situation is to accept, without seeing it, the religion created by humans in an uncritical manner. Any critique could be applied only to outmoded and dead religions of the past, which humans have abandoned because they no longer do any good.

So we can say that the "secularization" stemming from the rejection, or reduction, of the revealed truth is the opposite of the desacralizing of things and of religions stemming from the revealed truth. It is the opposite because the first secularization is never anything but the enthroning of new religions . . .

What we have just said concerning secularization/desacralization can be repeated in connection with religion. Everything being said about the opposition between the revelation in Jesus Christ and religion is right enough, but it is the revelation, not science or reason or modern culture, which destroys religion. Furthermore, there is no overlapping of those two procedures. There is, rather, a strict antinomy. The elimination of the traditional religions by modern culture is a process which creates new religions, and that is all . . .

In other words, modern Christian intellectuals, theologians, journalists, and clergy have made a gigantic mistake in their interpretation of the contemporary world, and that, in turn, leads to a gigantic mistake in the orientation of Christian and church action.

It seems to me that throughout the history of the church there have finally been three phenomenal mistakes, on which all the rest hangs. I am referring to mistakes more fundamental than the heresies, which were differences in the manner of explicating and understanding what was revealed. What I am thinking of has to do with mistakes concerning the relations between the church and the world, concerning the church's situation in the world. The difference is as follows: in navigation, one must make an observation, calculate the declination and drift, plot the course, and read the compass. If the compass is off, everything else is off. Whether one prefers sails or motor power no longer matters. In either case, the course is not what had been intended. Such, in my view, is the difference between mistakes of orientation and heresies.

The first such mistake can be listed as Constantinism. This must not be taken merely as an acceptance of the state and an agreement with the political power. From the outset it is an orientation toward wanting to win over to Christianity the rich, the powerful, and the control centers—which necessitated the creation of a neo-Christianity.

The second such mistake can be called the cultural mistake. It is the incorporation into Christianity of all the cultural values. By that action, Christianity becomes the receptacle for all the civilizations of the past, the establisher of culture and a synthesis of the philosophies—which necessitates the elaboration of another neo-Christianity.

The third such mistake is the one we are now making, that of believing that we have to locate ourselves in a world that is lay, secularized, scientific, and rational, and that we should build a neo-Christianity in those terms . . .

So we must be iconoclasts, but not of the statue of Jesus Christ nor of God. For the destruction of those statues, a conjunction of forces is at work. On the one hand, as we were saying, the word of God is taking the matter in hand, but the world is also on the attack. We can only applaud the destruction of the divine idol fabricated by Christian traitors, a destruction wrought by Nietzsche and Bakunin, but we don't have to resume their

accusations or dance a scalp dance around the true God of Jesus
Christ. That the God envisaged by Voltaire and that envisaged
by Bakunin are dying is well and good, but we have to take into
account that this in no way refers to the God—creator of the
cosmos, the God working miracles in answer to prayer, the God
of Sinai, God the Parent, the Almighty God, transcendent and
sovereign. To claim to do away with that God in the name of
Nietzsche's critique is, on the one hand, to apply that critique
where he did not apply it, and on the other hand, to confuse this
God, who is the God of Jesus Christ, with the rationalized idol
of Christian lukewarmness.

Iconoclasts, yes. That really means destroying the gods of the
world which Christians see without observing them. It means
standing up to them while taking them for prince charmings—
gods of the stadium, of speed, of consumer goods, of utility, of
money, of efficiency, of knowledge, of delirium, of sex, of folly,
of revolution, of agnostic learning, of politics, of ideologies, of
psychoanalysis, of class, of race, gods of the world calling for
unheard-of holocausts. The person who attacks the biblical God
in order to demythicize God and desacralize God, instead of
attacking these divinities, is giving millions of people over to
death, not only to spiritual death but also to physical death.
That is where Christian responsibility rests . . .

It is clear that the task facing Christians and the church differs
entirely according to whether we think of ourselves as being in
a secularized, social, lay, and grown-up world which is ready
to hear a demythicized, rationalized, explicated, and humanized
gospel—the world and the gospel being in full and spontaneous
harmony because both want to be nonreligious—or whether we
think of ourselves as being in a world inhabited by hidden gods,
a world haunted by myths and dreams, throbbing with irrational impulses, swaying from mystique to mystique, a world in
which the Christian revelation has once again to play its role as
negator and destroyer of the sacred obsessions, of the religious

phantasmagoria, in order to liberate humans and bring humans, not to the self one's demons are making one want to be, but to the true self God wills one to be.

At the mention of a struggle of faith against the modern idols, which are the real ones, I immediately hear indignant protests: "So here we are, being put back into the mindset of the Middle Ages. Ellul is inviting us to take part in a crusade against the infidels and, at the very least, to adopt a completely superannuated apologetic."

That would be a total misconception, not only a misconception about my thinking, which is not serious, but a misconception with respect to the realities. Crusade and apologetic are, in fact, institutions specific to the age of Christendom. There cannot be a crusade unless there is a *Christian world* facing a non-Christian world. There cannot be an apologetic unless the non-Christian is included in the problematic of the obvious posed by the Christian. No longer are we in that situation. To suppose that it is still possible to have a crusade or an apologetic is to be out of your mind.

What I am talking about here can have no more to do with crusade than did the rejection of "Caesar" during the first century of Christianity. I can't imagine the few faithful in Corinth or Rome launching a crusade against the army of the *Princeps*. We have come back to that stage. The fight of faith lies ahead of us. It is necessary, if we believe that there is truth in the revelation of God in Jesus Christ, as set forth in Scripture.

Surely that implies that the modern religions and the modern sacred are errors or lies. Of course, if we feel it necessary to reject all distinction between error and truth, that is our privilege, but then, for goodness' sake, let's stop talking about Jesus Christ, who is designated as the Truth. If need be, we could recover "Christianity" as an "ism," and make it into a nice amalgam of anything we please, but that is not what the Bible is talking to us about.

The fight of faith to which we are committed is not a fight against human beings. It is not a question of destroying humans, of convincing people that they wrong. It is a fight for human freedom. Reinserted into a sacred, a prisoner of myths, the modern individual is completely alienated in modern neo-religions . . . To smash these idols, to desacralize these mysteries, to assert the falseness of these religions is to undertake the one, finally indispensable liberation of the person of our times.

—ND, 209, 212–14, 224–25, 227–28

WHAT MONEY REALLY IS

Now, the Bible raises the moral problem only incidentally and gives ethical rules about money only secondarily. The Bible sees money differently from the way modern individuals see it. In biblical texts money is only rarely spoken of as a neutral object without autonomy or self-generated action. Scripture seldom looks at money from a monetary standpoint.

Doubtless it raises the question of the ownership of money, but only to attest clearly that we are not the owner. We immediately assume that the owner is God. Only one text exists that has this meaning, Haggai 2:8, but it would be a mistake to invoke it. First, the phrase "The silver is mine, and the gold is mine" is speaking of precious metals and not necessarily of money as a means of exchange and capitalization. We must get rid of our too rapid identification of money with precious metals. It is a coincidence, not a necessity, that metals have been used to represent money. Other civilizations which have used money, sometimes in a very advanced way, have not known it in the form of gold. Thus the biblical texts speaking of gold and silver do not necessarily relate to our question. But in addition, a complete reading of Haggai shows that this is a prophecy with an eschatological fulfillment. It focuses on the moment when the heavens and the earth will be shaken, when all worldly treasures will come to the temple and when peace will reign. Consequently, the meaning of this verse is not at all what we usually make it.

The other texts which speak of the ownership of money concern primarily the ownership of monetary symbols. In this category is Jesus' response to those who asked if it was necessary to pay taxes. Holding up a coin, he asks whose inscription it bears. The inscription indicates ownership, and Jesus, without discussion, grants ownership of the coin to Caesar, thus to the political power, the state (Matthew 22:17-21). A nation's glory is found in whatever manifests the reality of its power, and this includes its monetary symbol. Thus when Satan leads Jesus up a mountain to tempt him, shows him the glory of all the kingdoms of the world, and promises to give these kingdoms to him, he affirms that in the last analysis these monetary riches belong to him through Caesar.

But this problem of the ownership of money is still not at the heart of the question. Jesus raises the question in its fullness when he calls money *Mammon* (Matthew 6:24; Luke 16:1), an Aramaic word that usually means "money" and also can mean "wealth." Here Jesus personifies money and considers it a sort of god. He does not get this idea from his cultural milieu. Jesus did not adopt a designation for money that was popular among his listeners, for it appears that neither the Jews and Galileans nor the nearby pagans knew a god by this name. Jesus did not use a pagan god to show that one must choose between the true God and a false god. No doubt though, as Martin Achard points out, the way this term is used in the Targums and in the Talmud is already somewhat personalized. For some of Jesus' contemporaries, Mammon is one of the elements of this world which are marked for destruction, to be annihilated in the Messianic era. But we hardly see in this usage of *Mammon* the idea of a power, and it is certainly not a personification. As far as we can tell from known texts, we can say that Jesus gives this term a force and a precision that it did not have in its milieu. This personification of money, this affirmation that we are talking about something that claims divinity (whether Jesus adopted it from the Ebionite milieu or whether he created it), reveals something exceptional about money, for Jesus did not usually use deifications and personifications.

What Jesus is revealing is that money is a power. This term should be understood not in its vague meaning, "force," but in the specific sense in which it is used in the New Testament. Power is something that acts by itself, is capable of moving other things, is autonomous (or claims to be), is a law unto itself, and presents itself as an active agent. This is its first characteristic. Its second is that power has a spiritual value. It is not only of the material world, although this is where it acts. It has spiritual meaning and direction. Power is never neutral. It is oriented; it also orients people. Finally, power is more or less personal. And just as death often appears in the Bible as a personal force, so here with money. Money is not a power because humans use it, because it is the means of wealth or because accumulating money makes things possible. It is a power *before* all that, and those exterior signs are only the manifestations of this power which has, or claims to have, a reality of its own.

We absolutely must not minimize the parallel Jesus draws between God and Mammon. He is not using a rhetorical figure but pointing out a reality. God as a person and Mammon as a person find themselves in conflict. Jesus describes the relation between us and one or the other the same way: it is the relationship between servant and master. Mammon can be a master the same way God is; that is, Mammon can be a personal master.

Jesus is not describing the particular situation of the miser, whose master is money because his soul is perverted. Jesus is not describing a relationship between us and an object, but between us and an active agent. He is not suggesting that we use money wisely or earn it honestly. He is speaking of a power which tries to be like God, which makes itself our master and which has specific goals.

Thus when we claim to use money, we make a gross error. We can, if we must, use money, but it is really money that uses us and makes us servants by bringing us under its law and subordinating us to its aims. We are not talking only about our inner life; we are observing our total situation. We are not free to direct the use of money one way or another, for we are in the hands of this controlling power. Money is only an outward manifestation of this power, a mode of being, and a form to be used in relating to humans—exactly as governments, kings and dictators are only forms and appearances of another power clearly described in the Bible, political power. This comparison does not necessarily mean that money can be ranked with the "rule and authority and power and dominion" of which Paul speaks (Ephesians 1:21). But neither does anything require us to challenge this interpretation. Without proof to the contrary, it would seem reasonable to accept this identification.

—MP, 74–77

LOVE OF GOD OR MONEY

Although it is possible to say, following biblical guidelines, that the conflict is ultimately a conflict of love, a decision to love either God or money, we must be careful not to take *love* to mean a rather vague sentiment, a more or less valid passion, in any case a limited relationship. In reality love, in the Bible, is utterly totalitarian. It comes from the entire person; it involves the whole person and binds the whole person without distinction. Love reaches down into the roots of human beings and does not leave them intact. It leads to identification and assimilation between the lover and the beloved. Jesus Christ teaches us in great detail that our love binds us to the spiritual future of our beloved. This is how we must understand the connection between Christians and Christ, which is a love relationship. Love led Christ to follow us in our entire condition, but inversely, today it joins us to Christ in everything—his life, his death, his resurrection and his glory. Where Christ is, there also is the one who loves Christ. Such is the force, the vigor, of this bond.

Love for money is not a lesser relationship. By this love, we join ourselves to money's fate. "For where your treasure is, there will your heart be also" (Matthew 6:21).

Ultimately, we follow what we have loved most intensely either into eternity or into death. To love money is to be condemned to follow it in its destruction, its disappearance, its annihilation and its death. It is thus extremely important that we never try to justify, however little, an attachment to money or the importance we attribute to it. Nowhere are Christians told that their love for money justifies it or causes it to be used to God's glory or elevates it toward the Good. The exact opposite is said: that our attachment to money pushes us with it headlong into nothingness.

To the extent that biblical love is totalitarian, it cannot stand sharing. We cannot have two spiritual lives; we cannot be divided. We cannot "halt between two opinions"; we can neither serve nor love two masters. Because love makes us follow the beloved and nothing else, we cannot love two things at the same time. Jesus firmly points out the necessity of choosing. "He will hate the one, and love the other." To love one is not simply to be unacquainted with or indifferent to the other; it is *to hate the other.*

Do we really believe that if money were only an object with no spiritual significance Jesus would have gone that far?

To love money, to be attached to it, is to hate God. We can now understand why St. Paul says that "the love of money is the root of all evils" (1 Timothy 6:10). This is not a hackneyed bit of popular morality. It is an accurate summary of this conflict. Insofar as the love of money is hatred for God, it certainly is a root of all the evils that accompany separation from God. And in this same text Paul stressed that those who are possessed by this love have lost the faith: it comes to exactly the same thing.

But a person does not lose the faith over a simple moral error. It is always Satan's seduction that causes people to wander away from the faith.

But we are so used to minimizing the content of revelation that we think all of this is well within our reach. When we say that everything boils down to love, we feel very comfortable again, for we think that nothing could be easier. And we are tempted to say, "As long as we don't love money, everything will fall into place," or even to affirm, "I don't love money." Perhaps many Christians say this in good faith. But we must remember first the depth of this "bond of love," a depth which is beyond our reach, then that the love of money is aroused and provoked by its spiritual power.

Therefore, even if to some extent we are able to master our thoughts and emotions and thus the inclinations which come from our hearts alone, we still cannot dominate the love of money, for this is aroused by a seductive power which is far beyond us, just as it is maintained by a force that is outside us. This is what Paul reminds us of (and he is speaking about more than the power of money) when he teaches that "we are not contending against flesh and blood, but against the principalities, against the powers, against the world rulers of this present darkness" (Ephesians 6:12). It is thus not within our abilities to get rid of this love. When we are caught (as we all are), our force is insufficient. God's intervention is necessary.   —*MP*, 82–85

RICH AND POOR EQUALLY CALLED

In front of the manger where God's gift lies, the shepherds have come to worship, as we have ourselves. Shepherds, poorest of the poor—these are servants, half slaves, having nothing of their own, working for others, watching the flocks of others in the fields by night.

And the Magi, richest of the rich. We call them magician-kings, and this is not far from the truth. In their Eastern country they are primarily scientists and priests, clever in their understanding of stars, of mathematics, of administration. And little by little, because their knowledge was respected, they became wealthy, and political power depended largely on their decisions. Magician-kings, rich in intelligence, in money, in power. The poor and the rich, equally called to worship before the one who is already a sign of contradiction, the King of kings in the straw. King of these powerful Magi, and poor with the very poverty of these shepherds.

All have been equally called, each in the language that suited one, that spoke to one's heart and one's intelligence. Each in one's own tongue, as later, when the Lord established the church, each heard in one's own tongue about the mighty works of God.

These poor men believe in legends, in fairies, in the supernatural, in miracles. At the same time, they are sensitive to spiritual realities. They know what prayer is and they are waiting for deliverance. They know what meditation is (as all shepherds do) and are directly open to revelation. Thus God speaks to them in their own tongue, by miracle and revelation: the angels descend and call them. God gives them the sign which both satisfies and reassures them, which is within their reach: a baby in a sheep pen.

These rich men probably do not believe in angels. But they believe in their science; they know how to interpret signs in the heavens; they want to explain what seems abnormal. Thus God speaks to them in their tongue by means of the star, an incomprehensible sign. But it is impossible for them to accept that it is incomprehensible, for this would disparage the laws they know well, laws of science and of destiny. God calls them in their intelligence. He gives them a political sign, which also speaks to their concerns. Politically minded as they are, they know that King Herod's hatred for the baby is a struggle for power.

Rich and poor, equally called.

But the poor are called first. In the kingdom of heaven, the first in this world are the last to arrive. The shepherds arrive first.

So close to God's heart because of their poverty, they were right there, near the sheep pen, which is their own place. Jesus entered human misery, and those who live in misery find him only a few steps away. This does not mean that the poor are better, or that they can boast of being poor (when they do that, they become rich!). It means only that Jesus came where they are. And the revelation given to them is direct and immediate. It reaches them at the center of their lives. As soon as they believed, we find them at the door of the sheepfold.

The rich are next. They have a long road to travel. Wise men from the East, they went on a long journey. They crossed the deserts: deserts of the vanity of riches, of money, of power. They followed a difficult road with countless obstacles to overcome, some of which seemed beyond human strength ("Go, sell what you possess . . . And . . . the young man went away sorrowful; for he had great possessions"). They had to be patient with themselves, but demanding. They had to turn their thirst for knowledge in one direction alone, to use all the resources of their understanding and their wealth (for such an expedition is expensive!). This does not mean that they were more meritorious than those who had only a few steps to take. They were farther away because they had excellent human advantages. They learned little by little that these excellent advantages separated them from God. And since the call passed over these barriers to reach them, they also had to go through obstacles to reach him.

Rich and poor alike called to worship, each with what one could bring.

The shepherds, in their worship, brought themselves. For they had nothing else. They came with nothing in their hands, but they brought their prayer, their song, and their lives. They glorified and praised God, and when they left they became the first witnesses of Jesus; they told what they had seen and heard, and all who heard them were amazed at the good news. The first witnesses, the first evangelists: this is their gift of themselves and their worship.

The Magi, in their worship, brought something that in their eyes was worth more than themselves. Gold, the symbol of their wealth and also of all the wealth in the world. Incense, with which kings are honored, symbol of political power. Myrrh, used for embalming, symbol of the Magi's mysterious powers, perhaps of science. Bringing these gifts, the Magi put into God's hands the very powers of this world. They recognized that these powers belong to this baby. These rich men, having given up their attachment to riches, had to come so that humankind could offer God everything that gives earthly power. The poor could not offer what they did not have, but the rich could pay tribute with the world's wealth.

And this was not a purely spiritual tribute, for when these kings went away, they no longer had their gold, incense, and myrrh. They left these things in the hands of the Lord. They gave themselves along with their most precious possessions, for, when they went away, they also became witnesses—protectors of the small child that King Herod wanted to sacrifice. These magician-kings broke with political solidarity. On the way in, they had of course agreed to meet King Herod. Power met with power. They had mutual interests. But on their way out, they were on Jesus' side and betrayed their own interests. They no longer obeyed Herod and hid from him what they now knew about the true King of the world.

Poor and rich, equally witnesses because equally called. They were called *first*, before they did a thing, and their situation is the same. Each does one's own work. The shepherds watch sheep; the Magi study. They are not interested in God. God is interested in them and calls them. God calls them to worship, to offer up what is dearest to them, because God gives them, first of all, what is dearest to God: God's Son.

For the rich and for the poor, Christmas worship is self-emptying worship because God on Christmas night emptied Godself. God took the initiative and gave up power, eternity, Godself, to come to this place where we could finally see God.

—*MP*, 161–64

4

Christian Ethics

Jacques Ellul insisted that the foundation of Christian ethics was a relationship with God and a willingness to listen to the Word of God. For Ellul, the Word of God is not simply the Bible, but is found in a direct, existential encounter with the revelation of the Wholly Other. Therefore, morality cannot be systematized or dogmatized in any way. Instead, Christian ethics are best described as what Ellul called a style of life: an embodiment of the Word of God, grounded in one's response to God and others. Ellul emphasized that our fellow humans are never to be seen as a means to an end and should always be embraced with empathy and a sense of interconnectedness.

At the same time, Ellul believed that a rejection of violence is fundamental to Christian living. Throughout his spiritual writings, he continued to combat justifications of violence. He wrote that violence not only contradicts the spirit of Christ, it also mirrors the values of technique and the technocratic age. For Ellul, Christians should adopt nonviolent means of resistance and civil disobedience in their struggle for a more just society.

Ellul refers to himself as a Christian anarchist. He defined anarchy not as a lawless or ungoverned state, but as an absolute rejection of violence. *For Ellul, Jesus was the quintessential anarchist. By imitating Jesus, one refuses participation in any institutional and individual violent acts.*

THE FIGHT OF FAITH

In reality, the problem that confronts us is that of the Christian ethic, an ethic which has nothing in common with what is generally called "morality," and still less with the Christian "virtues" in the traditional sense. It is evident that neither a theological decision, nor an intellectual argument, even if it be based upon the Christian revelation, will enable us to know the Christian ethic. At heart, this is a fight of faith: individual, and in the presence of God; and a living attitude, adopted according to the measure of faith of each person, and as a result of his or her faith. It is never a series of rules, or principles, or slogans, and every Christian is really responsible for his or her works and conscience. Thus we can never make a complete valid description of the ethical demands of God, any more than we can reach its heart.   —*PK*, 20

GOD'S COMMANDMENTS

We must be clear about the meaning of the term "commandment." Although since Karl Barth the distinction is quite well known, it might not be entirely beside the point to remind ourselves of the contrast between law and commandment. Law is always objective, universal, neutral, impartial. It has a sort of independent existence. The law is established over against me. I am a stranger to it. It relates to me externally. It is present as a gauge against which I can measure every one of my actions, like a cold requirement which hangs over me under all circumstances. It is like a constraint which does not break my will but which does away with it by requiring in its objectivity even a complete submission. The law is an object, external to my life. It takes no account of the circumstances in which I find myself. It is perfect and serene. My death, my bitterness, my weakness and vanity, make no difference to it at all.

The commandment is the reverse of all that. It is a personal word addressed to me. A commandment is always an individualized word spoken by *one* who commands *one* who should obey. It expresses the will of the superior, yet in addressing itself to a person in one's individuality it takes into account the circumstances in which one finds oneself, the human reality. It is always formulated *hic et nunc*. It is always a circumstantial word, which is never a sort of permanent, eternal presence, even when it is God who formulates this commandment. It is always registered in terms of the concrete facts, and must necessarily be interpreted in relation to them. It is a person-to-person relationship.

To be sure, the law can be transformed into a commandment. It can depart from its icy majesty to accost a particular person in his life. In a sense, the Jews must have experienced this transformation, as is evidenced in Psalm 119. And in Jesus Christ we have the fulfillment of the law, one aspect of which is precisely that it is no longer law at all, but entirely commandment.

But the worst mishap is the transformation of commandment into law, the objectification of the word of God, or the legalistic interpretation of the commandment. What is spoken by God to humans in biblical history, a holy history of the walking together of God and humans, cannot be transformed into a law which is valid of itself and universal. Everything depends upon the commandment's being "made real in the present" (not by our efforts and our hermeneutical methods), that is to say, upon the commandment's being received now as real and personal by each one in one's own heart. The pronouncement, the proclamation of the commandment must be heard afresh, received as a new word spoken for the first time, by which God is speaking to me, and as something which I *must* now do.

For it is indeed a question of a duty expressed in a summons. I am called by the very setting forth of the commandment. The order is not of force in and of itself, but as a summons which puts me completely into relationship with the one who is calling upon me. When I hear that word I am not left untouched, with a free will capable of entirely independent decision. The command given me already starts me off in a certain direction. Yet for it to exist I still have to receive it for what it is, for the living commandment which concerns me.

The summons of the commandment is contained in its entirety in the Bible. But it does not cease to be a word for being "written" (hence objectified). It does not become letter, nor does the commandment become law. The word inscribed in the Bible is always living, and is continually *spoken* to one who *reads*. Thus the commandment to pray is constantly renewed. Throughout all ages it is said to each person, "call upon me in the day of trouble; I will deliver you, and you shall glorify me" (Psalm 50:15); "Watch and pray that you may not enter into temptation" (Matthew 26:41); "Watch at all times, praying that you have strength to escape all these things that will take place, and to stand before the Son of man" (Luke 21:36). Thus does Jesus command, after having drawn attention to the signs of the end of the age; and Paul, in the midst of ethical injunctions, writes, "Admonish the idle, encourage the faint-hearted, help the weak, be patient with them all. See that none of you repays evil for evil, but always seek to do good . . . pray constantly, give thanks in all circumstances; for this is the will of God in Christ Jesus for you. Do not quench the Spirit" (I Thessalonians 5:14-19). So prayer indeed rests upon a command. To give thanks is the will of God for us.

Can we fail to see that these words, which appear to us to be addressed to others and to belong to a time so long ago, concern us personally and are actually a commandment, since the situation they refer to is always my situation? Am I to be exempt from temptation, first of all that of sleeping when Jesus is in agony? There is the temptation of indifference, of loss of zeal, of alienation, and the temptation to give up on myself. Will I be exempt from distress, from agony, from misfortune, from despair? On

those occasions should I not remember Psalm 50, and the word
which has become personal to me because I am suffering? Am I
to be exempt from the call to support the weak and comfort the
poor, to be careful not to repay evil for evil? But if I accept that
as the meaning and content of a human life, how can I carry it
out unless I pray? —*PM*, 103–5

THE ETHICS OF FREEDOM

Freedom is the ethical aspect of hope. An ethics of freedom
can be founded only on hope and can only try to express hope.
Now it is easy enough to write or to find an ethics of love, but
an ethics of hope is rare. Usually we find only vague statements
about the need not to despair, about the trust we should put in
providence, and good advice about not committing suicide. The
gap which is to be seen here is due to common forgetfulness
of the link between hope and freedom, obliteration of the fact
that freedom expresses hope, and a failure to note that the one
who hopes is acting as a free person. It must be remembered,
of course, that hope is more than a vague hope that things will
be better tomorrow, or a stupid obstinacy that it will work out
successfully next time, or confidence in human nature that it
will survive the next test too after getting through so many,
or the assurance which is based on a philosophy of history.
Hope is none of these things. It does not rest on humans or
on objective mechanisms. It is a response of the individual to
God's work. Only at this level and to this extent is it expressed
by freedom.

Again, however, freedom does not spring out of hope *ipso
facto* or by a kind of necessity. The Christian does not become
a free person because one hopes. God produces in us both the
willing and the doing. Freedom is created by God for humans
and in humans. If hope is the response of human beings to God's
love and grace, freedom is the response of God to human hope,

giving humans the possibility of living out hope concretely and
effectively in daily life after a fashion which is not just hypothetical or sentimental. There is thus a strict reciprocity between
hope and freedom. God loves, humans hope, and God makes
free. Or, to put it in another way, God is the liberator and on
this ground humans are authorized to hope and to live out hope.
Because one has experienced the act of liberation this one knows
that hope is not vain. Only the free person can hope, since the
breaking of one's bondage guarantees all the rest. While humans
are still in slavery, there is no real hope. An external force has to
intervene, and there is nothing to suggest that it will. Recipro-
cally, however, hope is the virtue from which freedom can draw
meaning and which it is charged to express. If there were no
hope in the heart there could be no freedom.

One may thus see the difference between the freedom which is
in Christ and the movement of a freedom which derives from a
mere (if necessary) act of awareness and which taken alone can
only be a despairing freedom. Because this freedom is given by
God, it is not tied to the past nor linked to objective conditions,
not even to those which are imposed by God. For God gives real
freedom, and this is why God permits us to hope in more than
figures, signs, or symbols.

Our first glimpse of the link between hope and freedom is
in the struggle between humans and God, i.e., the wrestling of
Jacob, Job, or Abraham. If humans lay hold of God to get something from God, it is because the person has been freed even to
this point by God, who allows Godself to be seized and challenged and fought. At the same time the struggle makes sense
only if a great hope has been so strongly planted in the heart of
humans that they may believe that in this unequal contest they
can overcome God, make God yield, and bring God over to the
human's own view. A very strong hope is needed for the audacity
to push freedom to this extreme which is far more extreme than
that of Nietzsche.

We shall have to show that one axis of freedom is God's glory. The force which drives us on is hope of God's glory. Christ dwelling in us is this hope of glory in us. This leads us on to freedom. "We rejoice in hope of the glory of God" (Romans 5:2). There is no question here of glorification in the ordinary or human sense. We are to affirm in our freedom the truth of the glory of God which will be fully manifested. Our freedom makes sense only as it feeds on this hope. And to the degree that Paul speaks of Christ in us as the hope of glory, he is recalling that we are free. This is how Christ can be revealed in us. When the liberator acts to set us free, we know that he is Christ in us, and he also introduces us at the same time into the kingdom of hope, of that hope which is not uncertain or without object, of the hope which can be only that of glory. It is because we have the solid hope of glory that our freedom can be oriented functionally thereto.

This glory, however, is manifested only in the resurrection. It is a fact that our hope rests on the victory of Jesus Christ. In the measure that he conquered death it is hope for us (Romans 5:4). This victory enables us to put our hope in the living God (1 Timothy 4:10). If this hope is more than a passing emotion or an invention of humans, it is because in God hope relates to a life which can never pass away, to a life which has triumphed in Christ (1 Peter 1:21). This hope is connected with freedom, however, because it shows that the victory of Jesus Christ does not just place us in a situation of what has already been done. This victory makes freedom possible . . .

Freedom, as we shall see, must translate itself into the attributing of meaning. This is possible, however, only if there is hope, if what I do and see, and the situation I am in, have an ultimate meaning. I cannot impose this meaning gratuitously and theoretically from without. My freedom would be completely fallacious if it were expressed in a magical act of this kind. It would certainly be incommunicable. It takes on strength when it obeys the hope which indicates to me the meaning which God has given and which is thus possessed already by institutions, things, people, and events. This is why hope consists precisely in hoping against hope and against all the evidence. Hope is believing in the beatitudes in spite of appearances. Happy are those who weep—how foolish that is, for those who weep are unhappy and promising them consolation is a sorry jest. In any case Jesus says that they are happy now, already, at the present time. The one who weeps is happy now. This beatitude is true only because it is a word which God pronounces over the one who weeps. Hope teaches us to accept as true what God says and to regard as untrue what the evidence of the senses affirms. It is the direct opposite of what Eve does when she accepts the evidence of the fruit which she is offered. It rejects appearances. It rejects the reality which impresses humans when they regard it as a mandatory totality. Hope interposes as another and equally present and actual and far more effective reality the assurance of those things which are known by faith. Hope takes into account the solid and powerful reality of invisible things which faith can descry. It deciphers the signs which God has placed in humans and the world but which are visible only for and by hope. It creates open situations and shatters every closed situation. It breaks restrictions. It uncovers the meaning both of immediate things and of those that are still to come. It fashions thereby a specific life-style in the present. In sum, hope is the true and only hermeneutics whether in relation to the world or to Scripture. The rest is mere algebra and theory. But if hope authorizes a present style of life, this can be only the style of freedom, for hope, because it sees, produces a dimension which puts all forces and powers in their relative place. It breaks into the best regulated life. It can accept neither evidence nor the realism of appearances. It thus forces us to be free in relation to them. In particular, it brings freedom with regard to the means of power. The attitude of power, of control, of rigidity (including the rigid economic planning of totalitarianism), is a negation of hope. Where hope lives the instruments of power are devalued, whether they be political, scientific, ecclesiastical, economic, or psychological, and scope is given for freedom, which is itself opposed, negated, and constricted as the means of power develop. In the unity of revelation, then, the gift of hope corresponds to life in freedom. The ethics of freedom takes shape accordingly with all its uncertainty and paradoxicality.   —*EF*, 12–15, 18–19

THE WORD OF GOD

It is evident that the very terms we apply to God are contradictory: comprehend means to take hold of God in God's totality, to catch God in the net of relations we create. To define is to mark off limits for God, to grasp God as finite. It can't be done. Whatever we can comprehend or define is precisely for that reason not-God. God is, inevitably, beyond our comprehension, our definitions, and our limits. We can only point to God from the things we have seen God do. We can know that God was there after God has left; we can discover God's traces and recall God's words after their sound has died away. Thus we can bring forth signs of an ineffable and incontestable reality.

But we must not confer on these signs a value they don't have. We are not to make the Torah into God, nor the Bible into a "paper pope." The Bible is only the result of the Word of God. We can experience the return of the Word of God in the here and now, the perpetual return of the actual, living, indisputable Word of God that makes possible the act of witnessing, but we should never think of the Bible as any sort of talisman or oracle constantly at our disposal that we need only open and read to be in relation to the Word of God and God. And so we designate God, which is to be witnesses, concrete signs of what we point to. This is as far as we can go: testimony about God. There can be neither proofs nor demonstrations nor conclusions nor objective knowledge nor repeatable experiments nor a process of falsifiability . . .

God frustrates all our efforts to pin God down; God baffles all our definitions, but "gives Godself away" in certain words, certain decisions for (not against) us. God is not a subject except in relation to other subjects. And all the other gods are nothing of the sort. Consequently we can at best point God out and name God on the basis of revelation. We can designate God, give a sign of God, about God, toward God, a sign derived from what God has let us know about Godself. No more than that.

—*LF*, 190–91

THE END AND THE MEANS

The first great fact which emerges from our civilization is that today everything has become "means." There is no longer an "end"; we do not know whither we are going. We have forgotten our collective ends, and we possess great means: we set huge machines in motion in order to arrive nowhere. The end (by this I mean the collective end of civilization, for individuals still have their own ends, for instance, to succeed in a competition, or to get a higher salary, and the like) has been effaced by the means. Thus *humans,* who used to be the end of this whole humanist system of means, *humans,* who are still proclaimed as an "end" in political speeches, have in reality become the "means" of the very means which ought to serve humanity: as, for instance, in economics or the State. In order that economics should be in a good condition, the human being submits to the demands of an economic mechanism, becomes a total producer, and puts all one's powers at the disposal of production. One becomes an obedient consumer, and with one's eyes shut one swallows everything that economics puts into one's mouth. Thus, fully persuaded that we are procuring the happiness of humanity, we are turning humans into an instrument of these modern gods, which are our "means."

In all spheres the course of development has been the same. For instance, we must make people happy. In order to make people happy we must give people plenty of goods to consume. In order to achieve this a considerable production has to be organized, and then our consumption must be adapted to our production. But it is a very complicated process, for there are human obstacles and technical obstacles: the latter are gradually overcome by research; while the former have to be overcome by subordinating humans to the machine, to the division of labor, to publicity, to the use of one's powers without limit. Thus, the individual, alive and concrete, the "person-on-the-street," is subjected to "means" which are supposed to secure the happiness of "humankind" in the abstract. The "human being" of the philosophers and the politicians, who does not exist, is the only result of this tremendous adventure which brings misery to the individual of flesh and blood, and transforms the individual person into a "means."

This process can be seen everywhere. Another example comes from science and technology. At first humans felt it important to know the Truth; after the philosophers came the scientists. They elaborated their theories, while others applied them; these have been used first of all to prove the truth of these theories, and then for the use of humanity; from that moment science was lost. Gradually technical means became more important than the search for Truth. Science has had to become more and more effective for technical purposes, and now science is only significant in terms of technology. Its whole direction is towards applied science. It is at the service of means. It has become a means for the creation of more perfect means; and the abstraction called "science," to which homage is always paid, has replaced the search for Truth. This development is particularly evident in the United States of America and in the Soviet Union, but inevitably it is gradually penetrating the rest of the world.

Thus it is not difficult to see that the world is wholly given up to means. That which one hundred years ago was an "end" has now become a "means" in its turn, and even the "means of means." But a remembrance of it still lingers, because the situation

is so bleak that it is difficult to accept, and people transfer the ends
pursued into the sphere of the ideal, of the abstract, of Utopia . . .
This remarkable proliferation of means thus leads to making
everything "useful." In our world everything has to serve, that is
to say, to be a "means." Art and everything that is "useless" has
to give way to the necessity for "utility." Anything which does
not serve some purpose must be eliminated or rejected, and in
matters which concern men and women the same view prevails.
This is what explains the practice of euthanasia (for old people
and incurables) in the National Socialist State. Anyone who is
not useful to the community must be put to death. To us this
seems a barbarous practice, but it is simply the application of
the universal predominance of means, and to the extent in which
this fact is developed we may expect to see the introduction of
this practice into the whole of civilization. Then it will be justified as being for the greater good of humankind.

Further, as means increase, and as ends are relegated to the
abstract, they become implicit and are no longer questioned.
Everybody today is aware of the general aim of civilization,
and it seems futile and old-fashioned to ask questions about it.
Everybody has vague ideas about "progress," and it seems that
this notion of progress might be capable of replacing the pursuit of ends. People think that whenever there is change there is
progress, and in consequence we are increasingly approaching
that very vague and hypothetical goal which was exploited with
such romantic ecstasy in the nineteenth century.

No one is now concerned to question in what these ends consist, nor to see exactly in what direction we are going. No control is now possible, for the ends have disappeared, or they seem
to have no connection with means; it is the latter which now
occupy the whole field of activity, the attention and the admira-
tion of humanity. It is true that we still talk about "happiness"
or "liberty" or "justice," but people no longer have any idea of
the content of the phrases, nor of the conditions they require,

and these empty phrases are only used in order to take measures which have no relation to these illusions. These ends, which have become implicit in the human mind, and in human thought, no longer have any formative power: they are no longer creative. They are dead illusions, which are simply put among the properties of the contemporary theatre. It is impossible to take them seriously any longer, and no one would die for them. A person will die for one's own well-being, or because one has already become a means: the means of a party, of a nation, of a class, and as a "means" one is thrust into a battle which is being fought for no end. The heroism of a soldier in wartime, or of a worker in a strike, is in reality the heroism of a means which does not really know where it is going . . .

In reality, today what justifies the means is the means itself, for in our day everything that "succeeds," everything that is effective, everything in itself "efficient," is justified. The means, by being applied, produces a result, and this result is judged by the simplest criteria, e.g., everything to which we can apply the adjective "more," that is, greater, quicker, more precise, etc. If we can do this, the means is declared to be good. Everything that succeeds is good, everything that fails is bad . . .

The first truth which must be remembered, is that for Christians there is no dissociation between the end and the means. It is a Greek ethical idea which has caused this division. The point from which we ought to start is that in the work of God the end and the means are identical. Thus when Jesus Christ is present the Kingdom has "come upon" us. This formula expresses very precisely the relation between the end and the means. Jesus Christ in his Incarnation appears as God's means, for the salvation of humans and for the establishment of the Kingdom of God, but where Jesus Christ is, there also is this salvation and this kingdom.

Only this situation is the exact opposite of that which we have described as being ours today: while our civilization absorbs the end into the means, in the action of God, the means only appears as the realized presence of the end. The end, this Kingdom, which will "come" at the end of time, is already present when the divine means (the only, unique, Mediator) is present. The whole action of God consists in realizing through God's means the end, which is God's work. Whether this be the Covenant, or the Law, or the Prophets, or the history or the wisdom of Israel: it is always the same act of God which manifests this unity of end and means. But it should be the same in all Christian life; for the Christian also the end and the means are united in the same way; thus the Christian is irrevocably committed to fight with all one's might against our present enslavement to means.

—*PK*, 63–67, 70, 79–80

THE DEMOCRATIZATION OF EVIL

We are experiencing the democratization of evil. This statement will shock people. Naturally, I do not mean at all that democracy is evil. Quite the contrary! Nor do I mean by evil, moral evil. I simply mean the evil that we do when we cut loose, or the evil that we do to our neighbors when we overwhelm them with the noise of our amplifiers. Evil has many dimensions. But there is value in using the same word for this very concrete and material evil and for moral evil, for in effect the material evil that we do to others very often proceeds from the moral evil that is in us. The general idea is very simple. An increasing number of people among us are acquiring instruments that can hurt our neighbors or unknown people who, whether we like it or not, are close to us. This is the democratization of evil. Means that were once reserved for the powerful, for the rich, for aristocrats, and which constituted their privilege, are now within the reach of all of us. These means were always means of power by which the rich and mighty could ensure their domination and do wrong to the rest. It is very important to realize that these privileged means are now within the reach of all of us. This seems quite natural to us, for it is a democratization of comfort, of well-being, of a higher standard of living. From this optimistic standpoint it is good. But it is also a democratization of the evil that one can do to oneself and others. Previously only the rich had horses and carriages and could sometimes cause accidents to pedestrians and, as seventeenth and eighteenth-century reports tell us, do minor damage, splashing mud, scattering stalls, and breaking windows. But such things were not numerous, and they were disliked mostly because they were disdainful rather than harmful acts. Today most people have automobiles. And it has often been noted what a change comes over gentle and polite people when they begin driving powerful vehicles. Relations between drivers are always relations of vanity, scorn, competition, and anger expressed in insults and finally leading to fatal accidents. I could multiply examples of the same order in almost every sphere.

The democratization of evil involves two things. First, the more people reach a higher standard of living, the more they have means to provoke disagreements with others. Second, the use of more potent and efficient means of action demands people who are not only competent but who also have control of themselves, who have respect for others and take into account the effects of what they undertake. In other words, what we need are more moral people. To be sure, people in our society are no worse than those in past centuries. But they are also no better, and they now have more powerful agents at their disposal. At a very simple level, those who hated their neighbors might once have attacked them with a stick but they would have done so far less effectively than if they had a submachine gun. But everybody today in many different areas has the equivalent of a submachine gun. Think solely of noise. Extreme noise, as we all know, is dangerous from many angles. In the eighteenth century, however, the means of making noise were very limited. But today we can all swamp our neighbors with noise. People in the West seem to need an affirmation of their power in this way. In default of other means of satisfaction, they need to overwhelm their neighbors with noise.

We might refer as well to other areas of life. Pollution and accidents are the result of power placed in the hands of almost all citizens and their irresponsible or aggressive handling of it. The other day I saw an outboard vessel weaving between boats in a highly dangerous manner. A wave had diverted it slightly, and it struck a boat, damaging the hull, but it did not stop. We have to think of such possibilities which arise when drugs are readily available. Years ago they could be had only by the wealthy, by artists, and by half-mad intellectuals. Now they have been democratized and they recruit their victims among the people. This is the democratization of evil. We might also mention the ease with which explosives are obtained. A century ago attacks with explosives were difficult and dangerous. Nihilists were heroes who were ready to die with their bombs or dynamite. In fact we now find plastic and other explosives everywhere, and attacks, the taking of hostages, and the seizing of airplanes occur all the time.

The great writers of the eighteenth century who demanded democracy (Rousseau among them) all maintained that virtue must accompany it. This is very true. To grant people freedom presupposes that they will act reasonably, having regard for others and for the community as a whole, and not abusing their liberty. Institutions have never been adequate to make democracy work, to make people good, to prevent people from doing evil. But if this is true of political democracy, it is a hundred times more true of the democratization of technological means, their proliferation, and their placing within the reach of all. If violence is mounting in countries today, it is not because people are more violent. I believe they are less so. It is because they have much simpler and easier means of being violent. A weak impulse toward violence will produce very violent effects when the means of violence are multiplied.

If we want to make society livable, people will have to improve themselves. Moral progress is necessary. Political organization, economic change, or psychology will not do it. The actual situation shows us that contrary to what Marxism imagined, moral progress does not result from raising standards of living or bettering economic conditions or increasing the means placed at the disposal of all. On the contrary, these things simply trigger a frenzy of evil. The urgent need is not to establish a moral order, which cannot be done externally even by superior authority, but to find the way of self-mastery, of respect for others, of a moderate use of the powers at our disposal. This is the way of wisdom and morality. Such words are not greatly valued by our age—so much the worse for us! We have to consider that not taking this path will lead ineluctably to the impossibility of living in concert, a situation far worse than an economic crisis or war.

—*WIB*, 60–62

SALT, LIGHT, SHEEP

The Bible tells us that the Christian is in the world, and there the Christian must remain. The Christian has not been created in order to separate from, or to live aloof from the world. When this separation is effected, it will be God's doing, not the work of humans; this final separation will take place at the end of time, when God will "gather the wheat into God's barn," but the tares will be rooted up and burned. Similarly, Christians are not meant to live together in closed groups, refusing to mix with other people. The Christian community must never be a closed body. Thus the Christian is necessarily *in* the world, not *of* it. This means that the Christian's thought, life, and heart are not controlled by the world, and do not depend upon the world, for they belong to another Ruler. Thus, since the Christian belongs to another Ruler, the Christian has been sent into this world by the Ruler, and the Christian's communion with the Ruler remains unbroken, in spite of the "world" in which the Christian lives.

But this communion of the Christian with Jesus Christ has some serious implications: first of all, the Christian, by this very fact, finds that one is not confronted by the material forces of the world but by its spiritual reality. Because the Christian is in communion with Jesus Christ the Christian has to fight not against flesh and blood but against "the principalities, against the powers, against the world-rulers of this darkness." At the same time this communion assures one that one does not belong to the world, but that one is free from the fatality of the world which is moving towards death, and, as a result of this liberation by grace, one *can* fight against the spiritual realities of the world. To speak quite plainly, the Christian is called to break the fatality which hangs over the world, and *can* do so. In order to do this, by the grace of God the Christian receives the necessary weapons.

If this, then, is the Christian's situation, what part should the Christian play in the life of the world? It is only too easy to reply: to "witness," to "evangelize," or "to lead a Christian life," or again "to act according to the will of God." All this is true, of course, but so long as it is not really understood, so long as each answer is only a traditional formula, it leads us nowhere. Now it is the Bible which shows us what the Christian "calling" really is; it enables us to understand this situation, and it shows us what concrete action is required.

First of all, we need to remember that the Christian must not act in exactly the same way as everyone else. The Christian has a part to play in this world which no one else can possibly fulfill. The Christian is not asked to look at the various movements which men have started, choose those which seem "good," and then support them. The Christian is not asked to give support to any particular human enterprise, nor to the support the decisions of man. The Christian is charged with a mission of which the natural man can have no idea; yet in reality this mission is decisive for the actions of humans. For it is on this that the truth or error of human action depends.

If the Christian works with all one's might at some human project, the Christian is only a human being like others, and the Christian's effort is worth no more than that; but if the Christian accepts the specific function as a Christian (which does not necessarily entail material or effective participation in the world), this is decisive for human history.

God has not sent the Christian into the world for any other purpose than to fulfill this function. But this specific function cannot be compared with other human ends; it cannot be understood by the "natural man"; yet the significance of all other functions depends upon it. This function is defined by the Scriptures in three ways:

1. You are the salt of the earth.
2. You are the light of the world.
3. I send you forth as sheep in the midst of wolves.

To be the salt of the earth is a precise reference to Leviticus 2:13, where we are told that salt is a sign of the covenant between God and Israel. Thus in the sight of humans and in the reality of this world, the Christian is a visible sign of the new covenant which God has made with this world in Jesus Christ. But it is essential that the Christian should really *be* this sign, that is to say, that in life and words the Christian should allow this covenant to be manifest in the eyes of humanity. Apart from that, this earth will feel bereft of any "covenant"; it will not know where it is going; it will no longer have any real knowledge of itself, nor any certainty about its preservation. The fact that Christians *are*, in their lives, the "salt of the earth," does far more for the preservation of the world than any external action.

To be the light of the world: "And the light shined in the darkness and the darkness did not apprehend it." Christians *are* this light, through Christ; this may be understood in a twofold sense:

First of all, the light eliminates the darkness; it is that which separates life from death; it is that which gives us the criterion of goodness (that is why in the text this phrase is immediately followed by a reference to "good works"). Strictly speaking, apart from this light we cannot know what a "good work" is, nor in what "goodness" consists.

From another point of view this "light of the world" is that which gives meaning and direction to the history of the world, and thus explains it. In the succession of events which the course of history presents, there is no logic, no certitude, but this logic is supplied by the presence of the church, however strange this may seem. This is why, by being the "light," the Christian is an element in the life of the world; now, however, in addition to the work of "preservation," the Christian goes further: the Christian reveals to the world the truth about its condition, and witnesses to the salvation of which the Christian is an instrument.

Like sheep in the midst of wolves: here again the Christian is a "sign" of the reality of God's action. It is the Lamb of God, Jesus Christ, who takes away the sins of the world. But every Christian is treated like his Master, and every Christian receives from Jesus Christ a share in His work. The Christian is a "sheep" not because one's action or one's sacrifice has a purifying effect on the world, but because one is the living and real "sign," constantly renewed in the midst of the world, of the sacrifice of the Lamb of God. In the world everyone wants to be a "wolf," and no one is called to play the part of a "sheep." Yet the world cannot *live* without this living witness of sacrifice. That is why it is essential that Christians should be very careful not to be "wolves" in the spiritual sense—that is, people who try to dominate others. Christians must accept the domination of other people, and offer the daily sacrifice of their lives, which is united with the sacrifice of Jesus Christ.

These biblical phrases ought not to be understood as mere metaphors, as terms which we use when we are speaking of Christians. This language is not just a "way of speaking," a pleasant picture. We are only too much inclined to understand such phrases as figures of speech or as poetry. Nor is this quality of living something which "happens" to the Christian accidentally. People often say too easily that the Christian possesses this quality, but that the Christian could have other qualities.

On the contrary, all these expressions denote a stark reality, from which it is impossible to escape. Here Jesus Christ confronts us with the specific function of the Christian—and there can be no other. Things cannot be otherwise; the Christian has no choice, and if one does not accept this function, one does not fulfill the part assigned. The Christian then betrays both Jesus Christ and the world. Of course the Christian can always immerse oneself in good works, and pour out one's energy in religious or social activities, but all this will have no meaning unless one is fulfilling the only mission with which the Christian has been charged by Jesus Christ, which is first of all *to be a sign*.

—*PK*, 7–12

THE PROPER RESPONSE TO THE POOR

Are there not many ways to respond to the poor with kindness and good will? But this is not exactly the problem. The condition of the poor, we could even say their nature, is not there to arouse our interest or our charity (in the modern sense of the term).

This is no place for pity. Human pity can offer the poor only appeasement, falsehoods, and loss of consciousness. What realistic bitterness we find in Lemuel's words when he says, "Give strong drink to him who is perishing, and wine to those in bitter distress; let them drink and forget their poverty, and remember their misery no more" (Proverbs 31:6-7). This is all a person of good will can do for the poor; for the reality of human misery, the negative reflection of money's power, goes infinitely beyond human capacities. And in one form or another, it is always the same diversion and oblivion and loss of consciousness that is proposed to the poor, in hatred or in love, in religion or communism or comfort. It is the same falsehood, and we cannot accept it.

Giving money to the poor does not in any way change our relation to them. This is why Jesus reprimands his disciples when they wish they had the money that was wasted on perfume and that would have been better given to the poor. The disciples are wrong to contrast this wasted money with money for the poor. For money is not what will change the situation of the poor. Paul reminds us of the same truth: "If I give all I have to feed the poor . . . and do not have love, it profits me nothing" (1 Corinthians 13:3).

Of course, we must underline the *me*. Giving money to a poor person will obviously profit the poor person. But we have a totally erroneous idea of evangelical teaching if we think that everything stops there, if we think that all we have to do is relieve misery. No, for as we do that, we are in the position of the rich who pity the poor—yet who, in the long run, stay rich. Even their solicitude is not good for the poor, for the relation between them is always as described in Scripture.

But does this mean that there is nothing we can do? Our disinclination is reinforced by the idea that if the poor are truly the image of Jesus Christ, then they must be quite happy, so why help them? These are temptations: the temptation to run away from our responsibility and, more serious, the temptation to take the place of Jesus Christ. For only Jesus can say, "Blessed are you poor" (Luke 6:20). We do not have the right to say that to the poor. To Jesus alone belong the blessing and the curse; the church must not try to take his place.

Of course we must do everything possible to relieve misfortune, approaching the poor as if we were speaking to Jesus Christ himself. Here the situation is strangely reversed. For do we approach Christ as if we were rich? Yes, of course, for we crucified him; that is, in his presence we certainly did take the attitude of the rich. But when we proceed like that, we well know what awaits us. Thus we can no longer deny our responsibility. In approaching the poor, we are required to get rid of the easy conscience of the rich. This is especially true if we see the poor as God's personal question in our lives. Then the existence of misfortune becomes intolerable to us, and we will agree to do anything, to risk everything, to involve ourselves totally so that the situation of the poor can be changed.

But if their condition can change, does that mean we should work to turn the poor into the rich—and in so doing, cause them to pass from those who are pronounced "Blessed" to those who are warned "Woe to you, rich . . ."? For it never takes much for the poor to become rich. Once again, this is not the response asked of us. If, by extraordinary luck, we managed to get rid of all misfortune, to make everyone rich (first economically, then spiritually), then this "Woe to you" would ring out for everyone. Then we would pay for this universal happiness based on Mammon worship. There is no other possibility.

In this emergency, how should we offer the help that Christ's compassion requires? All we can do, like what Christ himself did, is a prophetic sign of the coming kingdom. It is to bring hope and grace in material form to the poor who are indeed under the Lord's blessing.

Here we find ourselves in direct opposition to Marxism. But the ideal is not always a synthesis which unavoidably emasculates Christianity. This opposition to Marxism is even more obvious when we consider that the Bible requires personal involvement. The question raised by the poor is not sociological, but individual.

It is not an economic question either. The only place in the Bible where a person thinks that the problem of the poor is *first of all* a question of the distribution of money, and thus an economic question, is in the example given by Judas. For Judas the important thing is to give money to the poor. It is to settle the economic question. But he thinks this way precisely because he is Judas. And his attitude leads him with relentless logic to sell the Poor One. This judgment and this perspective are just as valid today. All who wish to see only the economic problem and restrict the poor to their lack of money are ultimately the Judases of the poor, and are led sooner or later to sell the poor to the powerful . . .

The proper response to the poor will not be found in adherence to any group or program. To try to respond by joining a party, by accepting a program, by working at an institution, is to refuse responsibility, to escape into the crowds when confronted with God's question. The solutions that we think are a response, whether social, economic, or otherwise, are a dangerous lie. They are a way of getting rid of a troubling personal situation . . .

The only attitude that Christianity can require is personal commitment. We must take personal responsibility for the state of the poor; this is being responsible before God. But we are entering dangerous territory. We must not sweeten the gospel to make it acceptable. All we can do is measure our faith against the Word spoken to us, God's question which puts our life in question. To accept our responsibility is to enter into the spiritual and material condition of those who put God's question to the world. It is, in fact, to become poor ourselves with the poor, with the Poor One.

This is Jesus' very attitude, joined to our own. Paul reminds us: "Let each of you look not only to his own interests, but also to the interests of others. Have this mind among yourselves, which is yours in Christ Jesus, who . . . emptied himself, . . . humbled himself" (Philippians 2:4-8). Jesus' attitude conditions our own.

In the Protestant Church we have too often given up the imitation of Christ (one of the essential elements of the Christian life), forgetting that salvation by grace does not conflict with this imitation. James says to us, "Let the rich man glory in his humiliation, because like flowering grass he will pass away. For the sun rises with a scorching wind, and withers the grass; and its flower falls off, and the beauty of its appearance is destroyed; so too the rich man in the midst of his pursuits will fade away" (James 1:10-11). We are told here that in the presence of the God's grace and glory, the rich are stripped of their riches, exactly like the grass is stripped of its flowers by the drought. The first result of this encounter is thus the withering of the power of the rich, of their enterprises. They are humiliated. As long as they are not humiliated, we cannot be sure that this encounter has happened. The humiliation of the rich is the loss of their wealth. And all that the rich can justifiably boast of before God is to have been stripped of their riches, to have become one of the poor. They can boast of this, for this is participation in the very glory of Jesus Christ.

All this is just the theoretical formulation of the story of the meeting between Jesus and the rich young man (Matthew 19:16-22). There also the question of the poor is asked in Christ. Admirably, this question is also a response to anguish, to the human drama. The rich young man asks a question, and in response God makes him confront his responsibility before God's own question.

We see in this story everything we have described up to this point: material emptying ("sell what you possess"), spiritual emptying ("follow me"), joining the ranks of the poor without there being any social solution, without any amelioration of their fate ("give to the poor").

We must not be confused: the subject here is not salvation. Salvation is entrusted to God's grace, and nowhere are we told that this rich young man is lost; in fact, the implication is quite otherwise. The subject is our attitude, our life, our response to God's question about our actions and our concept of life. Here and nowhere else we are at the heart of the whole problem of ethics . . .

—*MP*, 156–61

CHRISTIAN ANARCHISM

There are different forms of anarchy and different currents in it. I must first say very simply what anarchy I have in view. By anarchy I mean first an absolute rejection of violence. Hence I cannot accept either nihilists or anarchists who choose violence as a means of action. I certainly understand the resort to aggression, to violence. I recall passing the Paris Bourse some twenty years ago and saying to myself that a bomb ought to be placed under that building. It would not destroy capitalism but it would serve as a symbol and a warning. Not knowing anyone who could make a bomb, I took no action!

The resort to violence is explicable, I think, in three situations. First, we have the doctrine of the Russian nihilists that if action is taken systematically to kill those who hold power—the ministers, generals, and police chiefs—in the long run people will be so afraid to take office that the state will be decapitated and easy to pull down. We find something of the same orientation among modern terrorists. But this line of thinking greatly underestimates the ability of powerful organisms, as well as society, to resist and react.

Then there is despair when the solidity of the system is seen, when impotence is felt face-to-face with an increasingly conformist society, or an increasingly powerful administration, or an invincible economic system (who can arrest multinationals?), and violence is a kind of cry of despair, an ultimate act by which an effort is made to give public expression to one's disagreement and hatred of the oppression. It is our present despair which is crying aloud (J. Rictus). But it is also the confession that there is no other course of action and no reason to hope.

Finally, there is the offering of a symbol and a sign, to which I have alluded already. A warning is given that society is more fragile than is supposed and that secret forces are at work to undermine it.

No matter what the motivation, however, I am against violence and aggression. I am against it on two levels. The first is simply tactical. We have begun to see that movements of nonviolence, when they are well managed (and this demands strong discipline and good strategy), are much more effective than violent movements (except when a true revolution is unleased). We not only recall the success of Gandhi but nearer home it is also evident that Martin Luther King did much to advance the cause of African Americans, whereas later movements, for example, the Black Muslims and Black Panthers, which wanted to make quicker headway by using all kinds of violence, not only gained nothing but even lost some of the gains made by King. Similarly, the violent movements in Berlin in 1956, then in Hungary and Czechoslovakia, all failed, but Lech Walesa, by imposing a strict discipline of nonviolence on his union, held his own against the Polish government. One of the sayings of the great union leaders of the years 1900–1910 was this: "Strikes, yes, but violence, never." Finally, though this is debatable, the great Zulu chieftain in South Africa, Buthelezi, supports a strategy of total nonviolence as opposed to Mandela (of the Xhosa tribe), and by all accounts he could do infinitely more to end apartheid than will be achieved by the erratic violence (often between Blacks) of the African National Congress. An authoritarian government can respond to violence only with violence.

My second reason is obviously a Christian one. Biblically, love is the way, not violence (in spite of the wars recounted in the Hebrew Bible, which I frankly confess to be most embarrassing). Not using violence against those in power does not mean doing nothing. I will have to show that Christianity means a rejection of power and a fight against it. This was completely forgotten during the centuries of the alliance of throne and altar, the more so as the pope became a head of state, and often acted more as such than as head of the church.

If I rule out violent anarchism, there remains pacifist, anti-nationalist, anticapitalist, moral, and antidemocratic anarchism (i.e., that which is hostile to the falsified democracy of bourgeois states). There remains the anarchism which acts by means of persuasion, by the creation of small groups and networks, denouncing falsehood and oppression, aiming at a true overturning of authorities of all kinds as people at the bottom speak and organize themselves. All this is very close to Bakunin . . .

For my part, what seems to me to be just and possible is the creation of new institutions from the grassroots level. The people can set up proper institutions (such as those indicated above) which will in fact replace the authorities and powers that have to be destroyed. As regards realization, then, my view is in effect close to that of the Anarcho-syndicalists of 1880–1900. Their belief was that working class organisms such as unions and labor halls should replace the institutions of the middle class state. These were never to function in an authoritarian and hierarchical way but in a strictly democratic manner, and they would lead to federations, the federal bond being the only national bond . . .

In my view, then, it is more necessary than ever to promote and extend the anarchist movement. Contrary to what is thought, it can gain a broader hearing than before. Most people, living heedlessly, tanning themselves, engaging in terrorism, or becoming TV slaves, ridicule political chatter and politics. They see that there is nothing to hope for from them. They are also exasperated by bureaucratic structures and administrative bickering. If we denounce such things, we gain the ear of a large public. In a word, the more the power of the state and bureaucracy grows, the more the affirmation of anarchy is necessary as the sole and last defense of the individual, that is, of humanity. Anarchy must regain its pungency and courage. It has a bright future before it. This is why I adopt it.

—*AC*, 11–14, 21, 23

JESUS AS ANARCHIST

The first event that Matthew's Gospel records concerning Jesus is not without interest. Herod the Great was still in power. He learned that a child had been born in Bethlehem and that reports were circulating that this child would be Israel's Messiah. He realized at once what trouble this might cause him and he thus ordered that all the children of two years and under in Bethlehem and vicinity should be killed. The accuracy of this account is irrelevant for my purpose. The important thing is that we have the story, that it was abroad among the people, and that the first Christians accepted it (we must not forget that they were Jews) and put it in a text which they regarded as divinely inspired. This shows what their view was of Herod, and behind him of power. This was the first contact of the infant Jesus with political power. I am not saying that it influenced his later attitude to it, but undoubtedly it left a mark upon his infancy.

What I really want to point out here by means of a series of recorded incidents is not that Jesus was an enemy of power but that he treated it with disdain and did not accord it any authority. In every form he challenged it radically. He did not use violent methods to destroy it . . .

When Jesus began his public ministry, the Gospels tell the story of his temptation. The devil tempts him three times. The important temptation in this context is the last (in Matthew). The enemy takes Jesus to a high mountain and shows him all the kingdoms of the world and their glory: "I will give you all these things, if you will prostrate yourself and worship me" (Matthew 4:8–9), or "I will give you all this power and the glory of these kingdoms, for it has been given to me, and I give it to whom I will. If you, then, will prostrate yourself before me, it shall all be yours" (Luke 4:6–7). Again, my concern is not with the facticity of the records or with theological problems. My concern is with the views of the writers, with the personal convictions that they express here.

It is not unimportant to emphasize, perhaps, that the two Gospels were probably written with Christian communities of Greek origin in view, not Jews who were influenced by the hatred to which we referred above. The reference in these texts, then, is to political power in general ("all the kingdoms of the world") and not just the Herod monarchy. And the extraordinary thing is that according to these texts all powers, all the power and glory of the kingdoms, all that has to do with politics and political authority, belongs to the devil. It has all been given to him and he gives it to whom he wills. Those who hold political power receive it from him and depend upon him. (It is astonishing that in the innumerable theological discussions of the legitimacy of political power, no one has ever adduced these texts!) This fact is no less important than the fact that Jesus rejects the devil's offer. Jesus does not say to the devil: "It is not true. You do not have power over kingdoms and states." He does not dispute this claim. He refuses the offer of power because the devil demands that he should fall down before him and worship him. This is the sole point when he says: "You shall worship the Lord your God and you shall serve him, only him" (Matthew 4:10). We may thus say that among Jesus' immediate followers and in the first Christian generation, political authorities—what we call the state—belonged to the devil and those who held power received it from him . . .

A further question is why reference is here made to the devil. The *diabolos* is etymologically the "divider" (not a person). The state and politics are thus primary reasons for division. This is the point of the reference to the devil. We do not have here a primitive and simplistic image or an arbitrary designation. What we have is a judgment which is not in the least religious and which expresses both experience and reflection. This judgment obviously facilitated the horrible lacerations caused among the people by the Hasmonean and Herodian dynasties and the ensuing uprisings and civil conflict. However that may be, the first

Christian generation was globally hostile to political power and regarded it as bad no matter what its orientation or constitutional structures . . .

I will briefly recall the story (Mark 12:13ff.). The enemies of Jesus were trying to entrap him, and the Herodians put the question. Having complimented Jesus on his wisdom, they asked him whether taxes should be paid to the emperor: "Is it lawful to pay the taxes to Caesar or not? Should we pay, or should we not pay?" The question itself is illuminating. As the text tells us, they were trying to use Jesus' own words to trap him. If they put this question, then, it was because it was already being debated. Jesus had the reputation of being hostile to Caesar. If they could raise this question with a view to being able to accuse Jesus to the Romans, stories must have been circulating that he was telling people not to pay taxes. As he often does, Jesus avoids the trap by making an ironical reply: "Bring me a coin, and let me look at it." When this is done, he himself puts a question: "Whose likeness and inscription is this?" It was evidently a Roman coin. One of the skillful means of integration used by the Romans was to circulate their own money throughout the empire. This became the basic coinage against which all others were measured. The Herodians replied to Jesus: "Caesar's." Now we need to realize that in the Roman world an individual mark on an object denoted ownership, like cattle brands in the American West in the nineteenth century. The mark was the only way in which ownership could be recognized. In the composite structure of the Roman Empire it applied to all goods. People all had their own marks, whether a seal, stamp, or painted sign. The head of Caesar on this coin was more than a decoration or a mark of honor. It signified that all the money in circulation in the empire belonged to Caesar. This was very important. Those who held the coins were very precarious owners. They never really owned the bronze or silver pieces. Whenever an emperor died, the likeness was changed. Caesar was the sole proprietor.

Jesus, then, had a very simple answer: "Render to Caesar that which is Caesar's." You find his likeness on the coin. The coin, then, belongs to him. Give it back to him when he demands it.

With this answer Jesus does not say that taxes are lawful. He does not counsel obedience to the Romans. He simply faces up to the evidence. But what really belongs to Caesar? The excellent example used by Jesus makes this plain: Whatever bears his mark! Here is the basis and limit of his power. But where is this mark? On coins, on public monuments, and on certain altars. That is all. Render to Caesar. You can pay the tax. Doing so is without importance or significance, for all money belongs to Caesar, and if he wanted he could simply confiscate it. Paying or not paying taxes is not a basic question; it is not even a true political question.

On the other hand, whatever does not bear Caesar's mark does not belong to him. It all belongs to God. This is where the real conscientious objection arises. Caesar has no right whatever to the rest. First we have life. Caesar has no right of life and death. Caesar has no right to plunge people into war. Caesar has no right to devastate and ruin a country. Caesar's domain is very limited. We may oppose his pretensions in the name of God . . .

[In] Jesus' face-to-face encounters with the political and religious authorities, we find irony, scorn, noncooperation, indifference, and sometimes accusation. Jesus was no guerrilla. He was an "essential" disputer.

—*AC*, 56, 57–59, 59–61, 71

NECESSITY AND VIOLENCE

Violence is inevitable, but so far as concerns society it has the same character as the universally prevailing law of gravitation, which is not in any way an expression of God's love in Christ or of Christian vocation. When I stumble over an obstacle and fall, I am obeying the law of gravitation, which has nothing to do with Christian faith or the Christian life. We must realize that violence belongs to the same order of things. And so far as we understand that the *whole* of Christ's work is a work of liberation—of our liberation from sin, death, concupiscence, fatality (and from ourselves)—we shall see that violence is not simply an ethical option for us to take or leave. Either we accept the order of necessity, acquiesce in and obey it—and this has nothing at all to do with the work of God or obedience to God, however serious and compelling the reasons that move us—or else we accept the order of Christ; but then we must reject violence, root and branch.

For the role of the Christian in society, in the midst of humanity, is to shatter fatalities and necessities. And the Christian cannot fulfill this role by using violent means, simply because violence is of the order of necessity. To use violence is to be of the world. Every time the disciples wanted to use any kind of violence they came up against Christ's veto (the episode of the fire pouring from heaven on the cities that rejected Christ, the parable of the tares and the wheat, Peter's sword, etc.). This way of posing the problem is more radical than that implicit in the usual juxtaposition of violence and love. For as we shall see, there is a "violence of love," and there is necessarily a quarrel between "handless" love and effectual love. Naturally, there are those who will protest: "But can anyone say that one loves the exploited poor of South America when one does nothing for them; and can anything be done without violence?" On the contrary, there is no escaping the absolute opposition between the order of necessity and the order of Christ.

But now it must be evident why we had to begin by declaring the reality of violence, explaining that it is totally *of* the world, and showing in what ways it is a necessity. For the Christian, if one is to oppose violence, one must recognize its full dimensions and its great importance. The better we understand that violence is necessary, indispensable, inevitable, the better shall we be able to reject and oppose it. If we are free in Jesus Christ, we shall reject violence *precisely because* violence is necessary! We must say No to violence not *inasmuch* as it is a necessity and not only because it is violence. And, mind, this means *all* kinds and ways of violence: psychological manipulation, doctrinal terrorism, economic imperialism, the venomous warfare of free competition, as well as torture, guerrilla movements, police action. The capitalist who, operating from his headquarters, exploits the mass of workers or colonial peoples is just as violent as the guerrilla; he must absolutely not assume the mantle of Christianity. What he does is of the order of necessity, of estrangement from God; and even if he is a faithful churchgoer and a highly educated man, there is no freedom in him.

—VR, 129–31

NONVIOLENCE AS THE PROPHETIC ROLE OF THE CHRISTIAN

But the main duty of the Christian nowadays is to urge the cause of the oppressed pacifically, to witness to their misery and to call for justice. The Christian should serve as intermediary or mediator between the powerful and the oppressed. The Christian is the spokesperson appointed by God for the oppressed. Those who are imprisoned need an advocate. Those who have been dismissed from the world's memory . . . need an intercessor. Was not that exactly the role Abraham played in behalf of Sodom? The Christian is necessarily on the side of the poor—not to incite them to revolution, hatred, and violence, but to plead their cause before the powerful and the authorities. If need be, the Christian must break down the doors of the powerful and declare the claims of love and justice. This role is much more difficult and thankless than that of a guerrilla chieftain or a corporation head, and there is no glory in it. To gain entrance to a corporation head and insist on discussing his workers' plight with him is much more difficult than to march in a picket line, for it requires much more in the way of intelligence, ability, precise information, and strength of soul. But we must demand entrance to the powerful because, in virtue of representing the poor, we are ambassadors of Christ. I hold that in every situation of injustice and oppression, the Christian—who cannot deal with it by violence—must make oneself completely a part of it as *representative of the victims*. The Christian has spiritual weapons. The Christian must state the case, make it one's own, and compel the other to see it. The Christian must—as we said above—create a climate of doubt, insecurity, and bad conscience. The Christian lends intelligence, influence, one's hands, and one's face to the faceless mass that has no hands and no influence . . .

One thing, however, is sure: unless Christians fulfill their prophetic role, unless they become the advocates and defenders of the truly poor, witness to their misery, then, infallibly, violence will suddenly break out. In one way or other "their blood cries to heaven," and violence will seem the only way out. It will be too late to try to calm them and create harmony. Martin Luther King probably came ten years too late for the black Americans; the roots of violence had already gone deep. So, instead of listening to the fomenters of violence, Christians ought to repent for having been too late. For if the time comes when despair sees violence as the only possible way, it is because Christians were not what they should have been . . .

Choosing different means, seeking another kind of victory, renouncing the marks of victory—this is the only possible way of breaking the chain of violence, of rupturing the circle of fear and fate. I would have all Christians take to heart this word of Gandhi: "Do not fear. He who fears, hates; he who hates, kills. Break your sword and throw it away, and fear will not touch you. I have been delivered from desire and from fear so *that I know* the power of God." These words show that the way Christ appointed is open to all, that the victory of good over evil benefits not only Christians but non-Christians also.

—*VR*, 151–52, 155–56, 173

THE VIOLENCE OF LOVE

The violence of love is an expression of spiritual violence. Spiritual violence, however, is neither acceptable nor possible except on three conditions. First, it must reject all human means of winning a victory or registering effects. I should like to broadcast the innumerable Old Testament passages which tell how God opposed his people's use of "normal" means of settling conflicts—weapons, chariots, horsemen, alliances, diplomatic maneuvers, revolution (Jehu)—and bade them put their trust in the God's word and God's faithfulness. This is radical spiritual violence. And God lets us choose. Paul also lets us choose. He tells us that he did not come "proclaiming the testimony of God in lofty words or wisdom," lest rhetoric and philosophy hide the power of the Spirit. I do not say that we are forbidden to employ human means. I say that when we do employ them (and we are not condemned for doing so!) we take away from the Word that has been entrusted to us all its force, its efficacy, its violence. We turn the Word into a sage dissertation, an explication, a morality of moderation. When we use political or revolutionary means, when we declare that violence will change the social system we are *thus* fighting in defense of the disinherited, our violence demolishes the spiritual power of prayer and bars the intervention of the Holy Spirit. Why? Because this is the logic of the whole revelation of God's action—in Abraham the disinherited wanderer, in Moses the stutterer, in David the weakling, in Jesus the Poor Man. Provided we reject human means, our spiritual intervention may become effectual spiritual violence . . .

Hence a second condition, consequent to the first. Spiritual violence and the violence of love totally exclude physical or psychological violence. Here the violence is that of the intervention of the Spirit of God. The Spirit will not intervene, will not rush in with explosive power, unless humans leave room—that is, unless people intervene. It is precisely because in this fight the Christian has to play a role that no one else can fill—it is precisely for this reason that the Christian can accept no other role. The Christian makes oneself ridiculous when the Christian tries to be a politician, a revolutionary, a guerrilla, a policeman, a general. Spiritual violence radically excludes both the physical violence and the participation in violent action that go with such roles. It is not authentic spiritual violence unless it is only *spiritual* violence. It plays its role of violence with, before and against God (the struggle of Abraham and Jacob) only when it refrains from any other violence. And this exclusion is required not only by the decision of God as recorded in the Scriptures, but also and to a greater degree, by the fact that the Christian can never consider violence the *ultima ratio*. We have seen all along that this is the argument regularly trotted out to justify violence. Violence, we are told, is legitimate when the situation is such that there is absolutely no other way out of it. The Christian can never entertain this idea of "last resort." The Christian understands that for the others it may be so, because they place all their hopes in this world and the meaning of this world. But for the Christian, violence can be at most a second-last resort. Therefore it can never be justified in a Christian life, because it would be justified only by being really a last resort. The Christian knows only one last resort, and that is prayer, resort to God . . .

So we come to the third condition in relation to spiritual violence. If it is true spiritual violence, it is based on earnest faith—faith in the possibility of a miracle, in the Lordship of Jesus Christ, in the coming of the Kingdom through God's action, not ours; faith in *all* of the promise (for the promise must not be taken apart into bits and pieces, in the manner of the theologians of revolution). This is a faith that concerns not only the salvation of the believer; it concerns the others, the unbelievers; it carries them and takes responsibility for them; it is convinced that for these others, too, there is a truth, a hope greater than revolutionary action, even if this hope does not attach to the material side of life. All of which is to say that there is a real choice to be made here (and making it will surely be the heaviest burden placed upon the Christian who tries to live out one's faith). We cannot, by taking neither, play on both sides. But if we witness to spiritual violence before the others, we cannot go on living in material violence, living for ourselves, protecting our own interests or our society. The choice is between violence and the Resurrection. Faith in the Resurrection—which is the supreme spiritual violence because it is victory over the necessity of death—excludes the use of every other violence. And it is true that, the Resurrection being accomplished, we can and must proclaim consolation and reconciliation. For humans today have much greater *need* of true consolation than of economic growth, of reconciliation than of appeals to hate and violence.

—*VR*, 168–71

5

The Dialectic of Christian Realism

In order to help his readers see reality clearly, Jacques Ellul made distinctions between the City of God and the city of humans, Christianity and Christendom, revelation and religion, and much more. This dialectical method is at the heart of Ellul's worldview. It is also the very path to transcendence of the hopelessness inherent in our present age. Only by recognizing these reciprocal counterparts can we see the correlations, interrelations, contrasts, and ultimately, the whole.

By perceiving this wholeness and living ethically, Christians can become what Ellul calls the presence of the kingdom on earth, bringing hope into an age of abandonment, while shattering the world's fatalities and necessities.

A DIALECTICAL UNDERSTANDING OF REALITY

I have found it impossible to join Christianity and the world into a single whole. From my very first writings I have shown that there is no such thing as a Christian politics that a Christian party can espouse, nor is there a Christian economics, nor, epistemologically, a Christian history or science, etc. In the first place, there could only be a kind of ideological cloak, and in the second place, there would be a deformation of methods and results. Naturally an ethics written by Christians can be a Christian ethics, but only Christians can accept it. Similarly,

Christians can study history or biology, realizing (like all scholars) what their presuppositions are and how they will affect their conclusions. Again, Christians may be members of a union or a political party and play their own part in it, but they will not pretend to be Christian politicians (something I have found by experience to be impossible and untenable).

From another angle, it seems no less certain to me that we cannot think in a Christian way in isolation from the concrete reality of society. Christians cannot live by eternal principles without reference to the real world. It is idealistic and fanciful either to think that Christianity can permeate or modify the structures of society (and here I come up against the function of ideology according to Marx), or, conversely, to think that Christianity ought to be adapted and modified according to the necessities, exigencies, and orientations of the world . . .

Thus I have found myself forced to affirm both the independence of analysis of contemporary society and the specificity of theology, to affirm both the coherence and importance of the world in which we live and the incomparable truth of revelation in Christ—two factors that are alien and yet indissolubly linked. Thus the relation between the two factors can be only a dialectical and critical one. Noetically we can only affirm two contradictions, pressing contradiction to the limit. Actively, we can only introduce the dimension of mutual criticism, the world criticizing the church and science criticizing theology, the church (as we should not forget) criticizing the world and theology criticizing science. Since the synthesis, the negation of the negation, or the appearance in some form of a new state can be only a product of history, there can be no question of presenting this synthesis in some arbitrary intellectual fashion in a study which will simply correspond to an appearance of response. I have thus been led to work in two spheres, the one historical and sociological, and the other theological. This does not represent a dispersing of interest nor does it express a twofold curiosity. It is the fruit of what is essentially rigorous reflection. Each part of my work is of equal importance and each is as free as possible from contamination by the other. As a sociologist, I have to be realistic and scientific, using exact methods, though in this regard I have fought methodological battles and had to contest certain methods. As a theologian, I have to be equally intransigent, presenting an interpretation of revelation which is as strict as possible, and making no concession to the spirit of the age.

If the final result is a dialectic, however, the whole is not made up of unrelated parts: there has to be correlation. The negative exists only in relation to the positive, and the positive only in relation to the negative. The two have reciprocal roles as in musical counterpoint. Hence it is perfectly possible to think in terms of correspondence between apparently unrelated works.

—*WIB*, 43–44

CHRISTIAN REALISM

Christianity does not offer an explanation that cannot certainly adhere with reality, nor an interpretation that will always appear artificial, but rather both an element of coherence and a view in depth. In other words, we do not at all lay over the establishment of facts a theory more or less Christian, edifying or not, but which in any case is alien to experience and would never satisfy us intellectually. On the contrary, we must first use the revelation that is given us to have a deeper, truer view of the phenomena than that which our experience, our senses, our reason alone can give us; on the whole, it is a new means of knowledge that God places at our disposal and that we have to employ concretely. Every simply rational or dialectic view leaves aside one important part of the facts: their spiritual tenor and meaning. Only the revelation of God can illuminate this background of history for us. But, besides, this revelation does more; it teaches us that the phenomena are never anything but the signs of another reality, of another existence. And it is that which gives both a sense and a coherence to these phenomena. Once again, this does not at all mean explaining them, but connecting them, because they are only the expression of a deeper reality that is revealed to us by God in Jesus Christ. Consequently, these political facts which we observe have a very much greater value than they could have to our human eyes, since, in place of locating an incoherent act within an incoherent history, we perceive the course of a more valid history, already achieved, already acted out, which channels, directs, and sometimes breaks the tumultuous, uncertain, but nevertheless irreversible flood of our human history. Christian realism is thus again at this point in total opposition to political realism, since it constantly seeks a reference to a reality other than itself. But this reference then leads to putting in place the political, economic, and social phenomena. And Scripture constantly invites us to effect this putting back in place. Indeed, one of the greatest present evils, with incalculable practical consequences, is usurpation. As a result of human usurpation of the divine throne, realism has led progressively to the usurpation of the premier places by all the material powers, and human beings find themselves dethroned, to the profit of the economy or of some technical application or another. Every power in the world seeks to usurp a place that is not its own, just as in the arts of today we see painting becoming magic, poetry becoming music, music becoming photography, etc. Now, political realism is in a way the orchestra maestro of this enormous confusion; it is what fosters all the aggressions, both economic and political as well as spiritual and cultural. The master of the demoniacal ballet reigning over a savant and technical incoherence with the consent of everyone. Christian realism teaches us, on the contrary, the existence of a definite order and leads to an effort to put [things] back in place. The model itself of this realism is the phrase of Jesus Christ: "all these things (economic goods) your Father knows that you have need of . . . . But seek first the kingdom of God and his righteousness, and all the rest will be given you, thrown into the bargain."

This shows us precisely the attitude of Christian realism, which will consist, then, not in a negation of one or the other aspect of the creation (what both political realism and spiritualism do), but rather in placing observed phenomena in perspective in relation to revealed truth. This very phrase shows us also that Christian realism is essentially active. It will never be a matter of mere talk, but rather of an effort to penetrate into reality and to transform, modify the course of this reality. Therein we are really then in the presence of an authentic realism. The task is not to understand, but to change the world. This idea, which was developed by Karl Marx, was essentially, and well before Marx, a Christian idea, just as realism is found to be, well before our politics, a Christian attitude. But because Christians had relinquished it, others took possession of it.   —*PR*, 76–77

THE TWO CITIES

The Christian belongs to two cities. The Christian is in the world, and has a social life. The Christian is the citizen of a nation; has a place in a family; has a situation, and must work to earn money; the setting of the Christian's life is the same as that of others; the Christian lives with them; shares with them the same nature and the same conditions. All that the Christian does in this world, the Christian ought to do seriously, because one is bound up with the life of other people, and must not neglect what are called "duties," since the Christian is a human, like everyone else. On the other hand, the Christian cannot wholly belong to this world. For this world can only be a "tabernacle," in which the Christian is a "stranger and a pilgrim." For the Christian it is a temporary situation, although extremely important, because the Christian belongs to another city. The Christian derives one's thought from another source. The Christian has another Ruler.

All this should be understood in the most strictly material sense: living in this world, the Christian belongs to another:

like a person of one nation who resides in another nation. A Chinese citizen residing in France, thinks in one's own terms, in one's own tradition; has one's own criterion of judgment and of action; one is really a stranger and a foreigner: one is also a citizen of another State, and one's loyalty is given to this State, and not to the country in which one is living. It is the same with the Christian, one is the citizen of another Kingdom, and it is thence that one derives one's way of thinking, judging, and feeling. One's heart and thought are elsewhere. One is the subject of another State, one is the ambassador of this State upon earth; that is to say, the Christian ought to present the demands of the Master, the Christian establishes a relation between the two, but cannot take the side of this world. The Christian stands up for the interests of the Master, as an ambassador champions the interests of his country. From another point of view (and here the relation is quite different), the Christian may also be sent out as a spy. In fact, that may be the situation of the Christian: to work in secret, at the heart of the world, for God; to prepare for God's victory from within; to create a nucleus in this world, and to discover its secrets, in order that the Kingdom of God may break forth in splendor. The Christian may be in this world, it is true, but all "ties" are elsewhere; all ties of thought, truth, and fidelity depend on God, and the Christian owes no allegiance to the world. Further, when we speak of "this world," we are referring to concrete realities: the nation, the State, the family, work. . . . To all this the Christian cannot swear unconditional loyalty. The Christian's first duty is to be faithful to God.

Now the two Cities to which the Christian belongs can never coincide, and the Christian must not abandon either the one or the other. The Christian may long to return, by death, to one's native city, to one's own country, but so long as the Christian is upon earth, he or she cannot possibly renounce the one or the other; on the other hand, the Christian cannot be satisfied with the fundamental dualism in which one is involved. In other words, that inner tension to which we alluded to reappears at this point; here, however, it is expressed in the realities of social, political, and economic life. The Christian who is involved in the material history of this world, is involved in it as representing another order, another Master (than the "prince of this world"), another claim (than that of the natural heart of man). Thus the Christian is obliged to accept this tension, this opposition, and the results from the acceptance of this inner tension—because the Christian knows that the two orders can never be equated with one another—that the opposition between this world and the Kingdom of God is a total one. But it is an intolerable situation, which causes acute suffering, and it is not a satisfying statement. The Christian can never regard oneself as being on the winning side, nor can the Christian look on with pleasure while everyone else "goes to perdition"; should the Christian do so, he or she would be lacking in the Spirit of Christ, and by that very fact would cease to be a Christian. Bound up with the lives of other people (by economic and sociological laws, and also by the will of God), the Christian cannot accept the view that they will always remain in their anguish and their disorder, victims of tyranny and overwork, buoyed up only by a hope which seems unfounded. Thus the Christian must plunge into social and political problems in order to have an influence on the world, not in the hope of making it a paradise, but simply in order to make it tolerable—not in order to diminish the opposition between this world and the Kingdom of God, but simply in order to modify the opposition between the disorder of this world and the order of preservation that God wills for it—not in order to "bring in" the Kingdom of God, but in order that the Gospel may be proclaimed, that all may *really* hear the good news of salvation, through the Death and Resurrection of Christ.

Thus there are three directions in which the Christian ought to act in the world: first of all, starting from the point at which God has revealed to the Christian the truth about the human person, the Christian must try to discover the social and political conditions, in which this person can live and develop in accordance with God's order.

Next, this person will develop within a certain framework, which God has ordained for the Christian. This is the order of preservation, without which, humanity lacks its true setting. Human beings are not absolutely free in this sphere, any more than they are free in the physical or biological domain. There are certain limits which humans cannot overstep without danger to the society to which they belong. Thus the Christian must work, in order that the will of God may be incarnated in actual institutions and organisms. Finally, this order of preservation will only have meaning if it is directed towards the proclamation of salvation; therefore, social and political institutions need to be "open," that is, they must not claim to be all, or absolutes. Thus they must be constituted in such a way that they do not prevent people from hearing the Word of God. The Christian must be ceaselessly on the watch—intelligent and alert—to see that this "order" is preserved.

But, in so doing, the Christian will find that one is confronted by two possible errors. The one error consists in believing that by constant progress in this "order" we shall attain the Kingdom of God. It is enough to remind ourselves of the Book of Revelation, or of Matthew 24, to condemn this attitude. The other error arises out of the conviction that by achieving certain reforms we shall have reached this order which God wills. In reality all solutions, all economic, political, and other achievements are temporary. At no moment can the Christian believe either in their perfection or in their permanence. They are always vitiated by the sin which infects them, by the setting in which they take place. Thus the Christian is constantly obliged to reiterate the claims of God, to reestablish this God-willed "order," in presence of an order which constantly tends towards disorder. In consequence of the claims which God is always making on the world the Christian finds oneself, by that very fact, involved in a state of permanent revolution. Even when the institutions, the laws, the reforms which the Christian has advocated have been achieved, even if society be reorganized according to the Christian's suggestions, the Christian still has to be in opposition, still must exact more, for the claim of God is as infinite as God's forgiveness. Thus the Christian is called to question unceasingly all that humanity calls progress, discovery, facts, established results, reality, etc. The Christian can never be satisfied with all this human labor, and in consequence is always claiming that it should be transcended, or replaced by something else.

In judgment the Christian is guided by the Holy Spirit—is making an essentially revolutionary act. If the Christian is not being revolutionary, then in some way or another the Christian has been unfaithful to one's calling in the world.

—*PK*, 44–49

THE MEANING OF THE CITY

As soon as the city exists, it polarizes all activity toward itself. There is something magical about the city's attractiveness, and it is impossible to explain people's passion for the city, its influence on their activity, the irresistible current flowing in unconscious waves to pull people toward its dead asphalt, without giving a thought for its force, its seductive power. Around the city there rises a wall of mirages, and on the map may be traced the zone of indecision where the individual can be part of the city's basic orientation without actually living within its boundaries. The individual assumes its manners, its language, its scorn, and its simplistic attitudes. The individual has its rhythm and bears everywhere, on one's clothes and in one's face, in the way one treats one's spouse and in the way one treats one's children, in one's work and in the air one breathes, in everything one is, the mark of the city. Even when one does not yet live there, even where one is close to the oldest country houses of the surrounding farmland, one is nonetheless in a locked cage. The city is not far away, and it is not hard to learn to live as they do there. And so the mores of the city are acquired, without its life. An invasion of the soul, hand in hand with the material invasion, the first wave preparing the mass arrival of the tractors, bulldozers, cement mixers, and air-compressors, announcing the heavy clouds of factory smoke, a job, getting up joylessly to a sunless sky and dirty air, air that is a mixture of gasoline fumes, coal smoke, and the immense breath of a million neighbors.

But no amount of reason, no amount of experience, and no amount of knowledge does any good: people stream into the city. They know that the city offers little of worth (although it can be shown that they are usually unaware of what they are losing) and that the city is past master at furnishing illusions. Whatever individual attitudes may be, nothing can resist the double attraction of land speculation and the city's psychic seductiveness. In the history of every civilization the same process is carried out: life becomes suppler and finally bends, ancestral customs disappear, modes of thought and mental make-up are modified, both the surest instincts and the most defective mysticisms are lost, and everyone everywhere is certain of the city's absolute material necessity. For a natural necessity, the necessity imposed by the weather, the rhythm of days and seasons, the city tries to substitute liberty, that is, the possibility for one to do what one wants when one wants.

But this liberty is a farce. The city must, in order to stay alive, have its night shifts, the accumulation of a proletariat, alcohol, prostitution (under whatever form it adopts, including the "very noble naturalism" practiced in Sweden), an iron schedule of work hours, the elimination of sun and wind. And it is simply false to say that we can do away with all this and still keep the city. This is the urbanists' illusion—very respectable individuals, but perfectly idealistic in the worst possible sense. For they have no conception of where the city is really going. They do not understand what makes the city necessary, and they believe that they can modify the city like a piece of child's putty. According to them, the city is freedom. But this liberty never gets off the architects' drawing boards. The city's path through history has invariably shown the same developments and the same powers in action. One would not call it a natural law, but neither can one see any reason today why this line of development, in the most urban of civilizations, should change. However, the illusions of the urbanist and the sociologist are easy to understand. For the evolution of a city and its role within a society, however often they may be repeated, can appear to be the result of an accident. They seem to be events that reoccur for no special reason, and things do not really have to be such.

Certitude can be found only in the position that revelation forces us to adopt with regard to the spiritual being of the city and its role through history as concerns the individual. The reality of the city, not as an event, but as a structure of the world, can be understood only in the light of revelation. And this revelation provides us with both a means of understanding the problem and a synthesis of its aspects as found in the raw data of history and sociology. However, we must not expect perfect agreement, for the two realities are not on the same plane. Although I cannot mistake the sun for the colors of the spectrum, nevertheless I could not know color but by the help of the sun. I could doubtlessly make a chemical analysis of the coloring agents, I could study all the physical or biological aspects of color, without ever having an inkling of living color, unless all these aspects are brought into play by the simple fact of light bringing out color.

So it is with the reality of human problems in general and with our particular aspect of life. Revelation—which was not given with this in mind, but which incidentally serves in this way—enlightens, brings together, and explains what our reason and experience discover. Without revelation all our reasoning is doubtlessly useful, but does not view reality in true perspective.

So when we said that we had nothing new to offer history or sociology, we were correct, but not strictly. We have in fact furnished no direct contribution to these sciences themselves; but what history and sociology tell us about the city is here confronted with revelation, is brought together and synthesized not as bare fact, but as illuminated by another source of light. And the result of this confrontation is the conclusion that the city is humankind's greatest work. It is humankind's great attempt to attain autonomy, to exercise will and intelligence. This is where all humankind's efforts are concentrated, where all the powers are born. No other human works, technical or philosophical, is equivalent to the city, which is the creation not of an instrument but of the whole world in which human instruments are conceived and put to work. All human activity is conceivable only in the city and in terms of its existence. All human works are secondary to the city. Just as Jesus Christ is God's greatest work, so we can say, with all the consequences of such a statement, that the city is the greatest human work . . .

Humans are not to be counted on to transform the problem of the city. One is no more capable of transforming the environment chosen for one and built for one by the Devil, than one is of changing one's own nature. Only God's decisive act is sufficient. Only the death of the very Son of God is sufficient to change the facts of history. Only the resurrection is sufficient to dispossess the demon powers of their domain. Thus it is only God, by God's act, who made the city into a neutral instrument. It is not completely natural that the city should be offered to humans in this way, for humans to remodel it, to recast it. The important thing is to know *by whom* it was offered to humans and to know what spirit will be dwelling behind the new face made for it by humans. For the city can in no case be only a body without a soul, only a pile of stones. At the very best, we can say that God opened a possibility for humanity when God offered humans this area God had neutralized by God's victory, and that God restores human liberty in this one aspect of God's work. But even this liberty is not great, because humans can act only in the name of Christ and by Christ, and because the demons are still hard at work even though the underpinnings of their presence in the city have already been removed. And this is where human work lies—to help bring truth and reality together, to introduce somewhere, in some small way, the victory won in truth by Christ into concrete existence, into the baroque, heteroclite, powerful materiality which humans are always accumulating, which the powers use, and which the victory of truth is to tear from their grasp. Such may be the true greatness of human beings. —MC, 151–54, 170

FREEDOM AND SLAVERY

At the moment when God speaks to human beings, this Word which is Love and Freedom liberates them at the instant when it reaches them and places those human beings in a situation of liberation such that they can hear and receive this Word. Freedom is an ethical situation in Christian doctrine. It is not located at the moment when human beings would be called to choose their spiritual destiny, at the moment of a decision in the presence of the grace of God. At that moment human beings are thoroughly slaves. From the moment when they cannot be liberated from Satan, from sin, from death, but by Jesus Christ, they are still slaves when they have not yet received the grace that makes them participants in this life and this death . . .

When we try to make more precise the rules of Christian life, to construct a moral code, a model that must be imitated and accomplished, we betray Jesus Christ himself. We despise this freedom that he acquired for us with such difficulty by his death; we fall back into the old enslavements, and we repudiate the title of children of God.

The Christian life is not a moral life, precisely because it does not obey a law, but it belongs to Christ, it is in communion with the will of God, and this will is not Law, but Love and Freedom.

One can also lose the freedom that is accorded us by grace by reintroducing into our life some other lord, by our submission to the Spirit of the World, which is always possible, and of which the epistles of Paul (especially the pastorals) give several examples. We alienate this freedom when we commit ourselves to a sociological current, to a social conformism, in pretending that it is the manifestation of the Christian life (e.g., the political conformism founded on a Christian political doctrine, adhesion to an economic system as an expression of the revealed truth or of love, etc.), each time that we justify with Christian motivations, for example, one of our political attitudes (almost always taken for motives of sociology or passions): we thereby cease to be free in Christ.

It is the same when we think we can entrust ourselves to an objective system in order to assure "the" freedom of human beings: when we think that political or economic institutions will give freedom to people and will render them free, when we consider *that the obstacle to human freedom* is, for example, one [particular] authoritarian form of the State or economic alienation, then we ourselves lose our freedom . . .

There is no freedom without love. This freedom centered on the desire of human beings, on their spirit of power, on their personality, is exactly one of the forms of this new slavery of which Paul speaks: "Everything is permitted me, but I will not let myself be enslaved by anything . . . " (I Corinthians 6:12), and as an example of this freedom without love which is only slavery he accurately cites the union of a man with a prostitute—that is, precisely the example in which a man uses his freedom while despising a creature of God . . .

It is like this because we are not freed except by the love of God, and because if we place ourselves outside of love we place ourselves outside of this freedom that comes from the God of Love. Without doubt it would be possible to demonstrate the ontological link between freedom and love, but it is more fitting, since Paul did not do it, to consider here only the theological link between the two.

There is no freedom except by the new relation that God establishes among beings, for in the old relation according to the world, with its connections of force, violence, and subjection, there could not be any kind of freedom, as we have in fact observed. Now, in the measure of this new relation, freedom is established for the choice of our behavior and for the direction of our life (as a consequence with regard to Satan and the Law), but this new relation is precisely that of love, which teaches us to seek the interests of others.

There is not more freedom when our life is not to the glory of God. Indeed, we would have to believe in freedom as such, in a freedom existing by itself, like what the revolutionaries of 1789 promised. But we well know that such freedom in itself does not exist in any form. To take the terms of Roman law, we are not "Ingenui" but "Libertini," not people free by nature and by birth but the liberated who receive freedom from their masters. And this freedom never exists by itself; it exists only with respect to the gift of God, only as an expression of the very freedom of God, as we already said, and actually *guaranteed by* God's freedom. If our freedom were not guaranteed in a true relationship between creatures and their creator, which has been restored in Jesus Christ alone, then it would cease to be. That is how we should understand the distinction between the free person (which we are not) and the freed person (which we will never cease to be). It is at each new stage that God always liberates us afresh. God does not introduce us into a permanent, durable state, an accomplished situation, but rather into a mode of being-with-God. If we pretended to the status of free people, our freedom would cease to reflect that of God, to be in relation with that of God, and would thereby cease radically to exist. If, to the contrary, we accept this mode of being that God chooses for us, then our freedom, always new, always young, ceaselessly points to the One who renews it.

That means that our freedom is not consumed by the effort to manage our life, in the intellectual or political choices we have to make; it extends much farther, it refers back to a higher freedom, it holds its value only in the measure to which it is the sign of the very freedom of God. Without that, it points nowhere, it empties into the void; it is a freedom without meaning.

But to reflect the freedom of God is to exist rightly for the glory of God. And when we refuse that, then we seek to grasp for ourselves what does not belong to us, we cut our freedom off from its root, and as a result of wanting [freedom] "in itself" we see it drying up and withering in our lives. We submit—subordinate ourselves, as a matter of fact—to our search for glory and power, which renders us slaves of the powers of this world, from which Christ delivered us.

Watch, then, lest you lose this freedom, Paul often reminds us; we lose it when we separate it from the charity and the glory of God. Here exhortation necessarily merges with theology. Why after all would we not risk *also* this freedom in the game of life? Because, Paul answers, you have been redeemed at great price. And when we consider indeed the price that has been paid by God to redeem us, then we become ashamed at the very idea that we might risk this freedom, which becomes the most precious value of our life.   —MF, 117, 128–31

CHRISTIANITY AND CHRISTENDOM

Christianity, on the contrary, consciously and deliberately produced Christendom as an embodiment of Christian thought. Christendom was to be an attempt to translate Christian doctrine into concrete, experiential, institutional forms. Just as the individual's behavior was to be a deliberate, controlled expression of one's faith in Christ, so the reconstruction of the state, the economic order, and social relationships would be an embodiment of Christian thought and reflect an interpretation of the Bible. Christendom was not a religious society in the sense that it was a translation into social forms of religious feeling that had always been present in humans. On the contrary, Christendom was the result of a conscious, deliberate process. How was society to be made Christian? Or: how was Christian faith to permeate every area of life, public as well as private? After all, the God of Jesus Christ was the God of all reality; everything belonged to God, including the economic and social orders. This relationship should be rendered visible, especially since the life of the individual too is a single whole and should not be divided into unrelated parts.

We moderns have a very false idea of what Christians believed in the third or the eleventh centuries. We are used to reading that the Greeks separated body and soul and that the Christians followed suit; we find the theologians constantly repeating the same texts about contempt for the body and the need for asceticism; we know that since the eighteenth century the bourgeoisie have turned Christianity into a disembodied wraith. Therefore we are convinced that this is how the Christians of every period lived and thought, right down to our day. Then we lucky people came along and, after two thousand years of error, rediscovered authentic Christianity and early Jewish thought. Here is ignorance indeed! And what monstrous presumption it has tricked us into! . . .

What Christians were really trying to elaborate, as they gradually created Christendom, was a social morality. They were more serious about it than we are today, because they courageously set about applying their moral principles and effectively modifying structures in the light of what they considered to be the true and the good. And they succeeded. If we read the moral treatises of the third to the fifteenth centuries, we find that they raised all the questions, confronted all the difficulties, and tried almost all the solutions we today conceitedly believe we were the first to think of. Naturally, they did all this in the language of their time and in relation to the structures and cultures of their society. Our first task, therefore, is to try to grasp what Christendom was. Only then can we ask to what extent it was genuinely grounded in the Christian faith . . .

Here then is a first aspect of Christendom: when Christianity assimilated all the sacral, religious, and magical elements in the ancient societies within which it developed, this was not an act of weakness or imperialism but the logical consequence of a principle. It is easy enough to criticize the decision and the tendency as based on a deadly confusion, which everyone denounces today, between revelation or Christian faith and religion. But I am not at all sure that these virtuous condemnations are marked by intellectual honesty. I am waiting for someone to explain to me how Christianity could survive while excluding everything "religious." When the kingdom failed to appear at the end of the first generation, Christianity either had to break down into spontaneous, short-lived little groups and eventually disappear or it had to organize for survival, and once it did this, the "religious" had to come into the picture. Then the challenge had to be faced: the kingdom did not come and transform the world in "the twinkling of an eye"; was this whole immense world that God had created to be left therefore in paganism? No: it must be Christianized; the world must be freed from the power of darkness and made to serve the kingdom.

This enterprise soon proved to have certain consequences. To begin with, in such a vast undertaking it was impossible to rely on the individualized faith of Christians. Not every member of Christendom could be a convinced believer who had had an experience of the Lord Jesus Christ and undergone a conversion or passed through a long process of spiritual growth. A dedicated faith and a corresponding lifestyle could not be taken for granted.

As a result of this situation two things became characteristic of Christendom. First, a person became a member of it by means of outward symbols (for example, baptism) and because of the supposition that everyone who lived within the boundaries of

Christendom should be a Christian. Because they served this purpose the sacraments were interpreted realistically, that is, as having an objective efficacy inherent in them *(opus operatum)*. Second, as far as faith was concerned, the Christian became part of a huge mass in which the faith and works of all who made it up were pooled, thanks to the church. Thus any given individual did not have to have a genuinely personal faith, for one would in any event be nourished by and profit from the faith of others, that is, of the church as a whole. In this scheme the church was conceived of as a body in which each member had his place and in which each would have faith applied to him, as it were (the "implicit faith" of the theologians). The very idea of Christendom therefore implied that a great many of its members were not Christians in an individual, personal way. To say that medieval society was a Christendom is to say, not that all its members had a personal internalized faith in Jesus Christ, but simply that all profited from the faith common to the body as a whole.

This attitude necessarily tended to turn Christianity into an ideology; that is, Christianity became a set of presuppositions that determined the life of the collectivity. It was taken for granted that every individual was meant to be a Christian (how could one be anything else?) and that one became a Christian in a full and unqualified way through baptism. Christianity provided a scale of shared values, a store of patterns for behavior and attitudes, a set of ready-made ideas and of goals, norms of judgment, and reference points for evaluating words, feelings, thoughts, and actions. Here, then, was belief based on social fact; belief that was generally accepted yet no longer implied a total self-giving or a high degree of fervor. This did not mean, of course, that individuals did not sincerely accept the truths of the gospel, although the latter had to be transposed to a lower register, as it were, so as to be accessible to all.

A second consequence of the vast enterprise which Christendom represented was formalism. Everybody had become

Christian, every citizen of Christendom was a Christian. Therefore there was no need to evaluate inner spiritual authenticity;
the important thing was how a person acted. Morality was primary. The compiling of the sixth-century Irish penitential books
was a critical factor in this development. Soon, moreover, concern for morality became concern for law.

The church of Christendom would soon be characterized by
its concern for morality (a very legitimate concern in western
society between the third and eleventh centuries when the moral
corruption was so great that anyone not a professional theologian will have difficulty in imagining it) and by its striving
for organization. Morality and organization were necessary if
the vast totality called Christendom were not to fall apart but
were to function properly. But a theological principle was also at
work in this functioning. Faith was taken for granted; attention
could therefore be turned to the works which had their origin
in faith. But, at the same time, it was possible to influence the
presumed "implicit faith" through these same works. In other
words, rectify and Christianize people's behavior and you have
indirect access to their faith itself. The aim, therefore, was not to
arouse or control faith directly, but to stimulate it by controlling
its outward expressions. Once this approach was adopted, all
behavior had to be precisely and unambiguously described,
measured, and circumscribed. Models of behavior had to be
provided and aberrant behavior condemned; patterns of organization for the church and for everyday life had to be established
and prohibited areas clearly marked off. The church was on the
way to becoming a great ethico-juridical organism.

—ND, 2–8

THE SUBVERSION OF CHRISTIANITY

The question that I want to sketch in this work is one that trou-
bles me most deeply. As I now see it, it seems to be insoluble
and assumes a serious character of historical oddness. It may be

put very simply: How has it come about that the development
of Christianity and the church has given birth to a society, a
civilization, a culture that are completely opposite to what we
read in the Bible, to what is indisputably the text of the law, the
prophets, Jesus, and Paul? I say advisedly "completely opposite."
There is not just contradiction on one point but on all points.
On the one hand, Christianity has been accused of a whole list
of faults, crimes, and deceptions that are nowhere to be found in
the original text and inspiration. On the other hand, revelation
has been progressively modeled and reinterpreted according to
the practice of Christianity and the church. Critics have been
unwilling to consider anything but this practice, this concrete
reality, absolutely refusing to refer to the truth of what is said.
There is not just deviation but radical and essential contradiction, or real subversion . . .

We have to admit that there is an immeasurable distance
between all that we read in the Bible and the practice of the
church and Christians. This is why I can speak validly of perversion or subversion, for, as I shall show, practice has been the
total opposite of what is required of us. As I see it, this is the
unanswerable question that Kierkegaard faced in his day. He
replied to it in his own way. Today we must attempt something
different. We must follow a different path and take up again this
searching of conscience . . .

The question remains all the same. If the Holy Spirit is and
has been with Christians and the churches, we should not have
seen the terrible subversion that has substituted the exact opposite for Christianity, or rather for the X of God, replacing it with
a Christianity that is remodeled by the world. Are we to believe,
then, that God has withdrawn and is silent? I tried to say something of the kind in my *L'Espérance oubliée*. Are we to think that
God has failed? But the failure of a Christianity that expresses
what we have made of revelation does not change at all what
God has accomplished. God became incarnate. Jesus Christ, the
Son, died (and our sins are pardoned). Christ is risen (and death,

chaos, and the devil are defeated). No matter what may be the mischances of history or the errors and aberrations of the human race, these things endure. What is done is done. Irrespective of what we make of Christianity, God's work and accomplishment are complete, and they are inscribed in human history.

The question, however, concerns what we have made of them. Now by the Holy Spirit they have an impact in history. But the Holy Spirit is no more dictatorial, authoritarian, automatic, or autosufficient than the Word of God or Jesus Christ. The Holy Spirit *liberates*. Where the Spirit of the Lord is, there is freedom. In other words, no constraint weighs on us to make us do as God has decided. On the contrary, the Spirit is a power that liberates us from every bondage and puts us in a situation of freedom, choice, and open possibilities. The Spirit is a power of truth illuminating us and giving us a new and profound outlook on God and the world. The Spirit is a power that augments human action when we choose to do God's will. The Spirit is finally a power of conscience showing us what God's will is (the Spirit leads into all truth), that is, preventing us, when we are converted and illumined by the Holy Spirit, from seeking final refuge in ignorance. The Spirit makes possible a full awareness of the value and reach of our practice. The Spirit makes us fully responsible. This is the result of the presence of the Holy Spirit.

In fabricating Christianity, therefore, Christians have known what they were doing. They have freely chosen this course. They have voluntarily forsaken revelation and God. They have opted for new bondage. They have not aspired to the full gift of the Holy Spirit that would have enabled them to take the new way that God opened up. They have made a different choice and left the Holy Spirit unemployed, idle, present only on sufferance. This is why the burning question is a purely human one: Why have Christians taken this contrary course? What forces, mechanisms, stakes, strategies, or structures have induced this subversion? For human aggrandizement and nothing else . . .

What has been the result? A Christianity that is itself a religion. The best, it might be said, the peak of religious history. A religion classed as monotheistic. A religion marked by all the traits of religion: myths, legends, rites, holy things, beliefs, clergy, etc. A Christianity that has fashioned a morality—and what a morality!—the most strict, the most moralistic, the most debilitating, the one that most reduces adherents to infants and renders them irresponsible, or, if I were to be malicious, I should say the one that makes of them happy imbeciles, who are sure of their salvation if they obey this morality, a morality that consists of chastity, absolute obedience (which in unheard-of fashions ends up as the supreme value in Christianity), sacrifice, etc. A Christianity that has become totally conservative in every domain—political, economic, social, etc.—which nothing can budge or change. Political power, that is good. Whatever challenges or criticizes it, that is evil.   —*SC*, 3, 7, 12–3, 17

RELIGION AND REVELATION

The opposition between religion and revelation can really be understood quite simply, and before working out its consequences, we can reduce it to a maxim: religion goes up, revelation comes down. Once you have truly grasped this, you have the key to the problem.

From the very beginning humankind has sought to go up. Religion was at the same time both the principal instrument of this ascent and its expression, perhaps its origin. When Adam finds himself in Eden, he tries to ascend to the level of God. When people gather to attend to their common work, they are essentially building the city, but that includes the Tower of Babel, climbing to the heavens . . .

On the basis, then, of this natural need or sentiment, people build up whole edifices of their various religions. *Re-ligare*, "rebind, attach": religion attaches us, whether to the past or to eternity, to our ancestors or the gods. But it also links us to the living human community and serves to bond society together, a point we shall be returning to.

It's also possible to connect "religion" to *re-legere*, "reread," which brings us to the other great edifice, myth and ritual—the rereading, repetition, and reproduction of the foundational word, the rite, the self-empowered formula. Here we have the recitation of the primordial myth, the explanation of the world's origins which at the same time holds the key to its end. And projecting outward from this rereading or "binding" is the structure composed of priests, ceremonies, temples and offerings, sacrifices and patterns of conduct: the whole religious "system."

I don't think there's anything excessive or out of order in the foregoing passage. I'm trying to show that religious systems are perfectly natural and consistent with human behavior. But we also have to recall the purely sociological side of religion, religion as an indispensable and most economical means of assuring the unity of a group. The religious bond makes it possible to establish complex group structures considered by their members as inevitable. And there is always a connection with something "higher," whether it be a higher order or a higher being. The structure of society can be either the reflection, the replica of that heavenly order or the expression of a commandment, with the divinity prescribing the various hierarchies and kinds of relationships.

We must remember that there is no dispensing with this organization. There is no society or even community anywhere that lives without rules or government, operating simply on the basis of continual spontaneous desire. Thus religion is at once the expression of individual need and the appropriate instrument of social logic. It specifies both origins and ends. Religion is the most economical mode of social bonding, and at the same time it vouches to the members of society for the validity and legitimacy of the rules they obey. Consider how, as soon as religious feelings slacken, the law, for example, loses so much of its weight and authority. It's not necessary for law to be directly inspired by a divine source; it need only be connected to that source . . .

But we are filled with stupefaction when we realize that in every aspect the revelation of the God of Abraham, Isaac, and Jacob, of the God of Jesus Christ, is exactly and entirely contrary to what we have just described. The central fact, the crucial point, is that here God descends to humans. Never in any way, under any circumstances can we ascend to God, howsoever slightly. God has chosen to descend and to put Godself on our level. It's not just that God expressly declares in the story of the Tower of Babel, "Let us go down." And yet the myth is very clear: people build the tower to climb up and enter into contact with God, to equal God, to get hold of God, and whatever else one can imagine. In the face of this God proclaims God's intention to go down and see.

The lofty intellectual will smile at such a childish phrase, at a God who needs to descend, to get closer in order "to see." But it's the clever intellectual who is childish. The important thing here is to stress the disjunction: the religious person wants to go up, but the God of the Bible is a God who comes down, and it is on this God that revelation (which is thus contrary to religion) finally rests. I would go so far as to say that *this* is what revelation is all about . . .

Now this downward movement of revelation entails a number of radical consequences, which are precisely the opposite of those brought on by the ascending movement of religion. Revelation leads to the affirmation of powerlessness, the destabilization of human communities, the shattering of unity, the invalidating of law, and the impossibility of establishing an explicit, definitive content of faith. In that religion ascends, it always expresses itself in a show of power; and when religion has God enter the scene, it's always for the purpose of having a little more power. On the contrary, as we have to keep repeating, the revelation of

God guides humans in the direction of powerlessness, toward the choice to abandon human means of domination in order to become a people that entrusts itself in God's hands, to the free decision—and the free grace—of that God.

—*LF*, 129, 132–33, 137–38, 141–142

THE IMAGE AND THE WORD

The omnipresence of images, however, is not an accidental, sporadic, changeable fact. We are dealing instead with an almost total milieu in which all of existence unfolds more or less smoothly. Truly it is a *universe* of images in the midst of which we are set as spectators. Our eyes' function has been extraordinarily expanded. Our brain is constantly receiving the impact of imaginary sights and no longer of reality. Today we can no longer live without the reference and diversion provided by images. For a large proportion of our lives we live as mere spectators. Until the present time our perception of reality through sight incited us to action. But now the superficial spectacle imposes itself on us all day long, turning us into passive recorders of images. This multiplication of images comes together in such a tight weave that we are hopelessly hemmed in, and everyone feels a need for images. These factors make it plain that we are not dealing here with chance but with a precise progression.

Images are the chosen form of expression in our civilization—images, not words. For though our era speaks, and abounds in printed paper, so that written thought has never been as widespread as today, still there is a strange movement that deprives the word of its importance. Talk and newspapers are like word mills to which no one attaches any importance anymore. Who would still consider a book as something decisive and capable of changing one's life, when there are so many of them? And a person's word, buried under the floods of millions of people's words, no longer has any meaning or outreach. The word has no importance for any listener because it is broadcast in millions of instances over thousands of miles . . .

Sight triumphs because it is useful. The deluge of artificial, superabundant images creates a new world environment. Sight saves us the trouble of thinking and having to remember. It lets us live on the basis of representation and substitution. It reinforces a group's cohesiveness. The word divides, whereas images (when consciously organized) unite, as for example in liturgy.

Artificial images provide another example of that movement so often described in which, as discoveries take place, we assign to some mechanism or other a quality which was a part of our human uniqueness. The most extreme example is the computer, which is even called on to "think" in our place. Because I have my photograph album I no longer need remember. I no longer need the slow process of reflection, since I function on the basis of evidence. I no longer need to search so hard for ways of living in community, because communion is established by the image's all-encompassing identity. Techniques replace me in a growing number of activities, and the universe of images to which I belong facilitates this substitution to an incredible degree.

Images are indispensable for the construction of the technological society. If we remained at the stage of verbal dialogue, inevitably we would be led to critical reflection. But images exclude criticism. The habit of living in this image-oriented world leads me to give up dialectical thought and criticism. It is so much easier to give up and let myself be carried along by the continually renewed wave of images. They provide me from moment to moment with exactly the amount of stimulus I need. They give me the emotional level (the anger, the tender feelings, and the degree of interest) that I can tolerate and find indispensable in this gray world. Images are essential if I am to avoid seeing the day-to-day reality I live in. They glitter continuously around me, allowing me to live in a sort of image-oriented fantasy.

Images are also indispensable as a form of compensation. The word would only increases my anxiety and uncertainty. It would make me more conscious of my emptiness, my impotence, and the insignificance of my situation. With images, however, everything unpleasant is erased and my drab existence decorated by their charm and sparkle.

Above all, I must not become aware of reality, so images create a substitute reality. The word obliges me to consider reality from the point of view of truth. Artificial images, passing themselves off for truth, obliterate and erase the reality of my life and my society. They allow me to enter an image-filled reality that is much more thrilling. Even television news, when it deals with catastrophes, disasters, and crises, takes the drama out of them by making them extraordinary and thrilling—by literally converting them into something metaphysical. The more terrible the spectacle, the calmer the hypnosis of the images makes me.

—*HW*, 126–28

THE WORD: DIALOGUE, PARADOX, AND MYSTERY

This brings us to the distinctives that characterize only the word: discussion, paradox, and mystery. Language is always unobtrusive, even when it tries to be demonstrative. It includes an unknown aspect in the background that makes it something secret and revealed. Language is unobtrusive in that it never asserts itself on its own. When it uses a loudspeaker and crushes others with its powerful equipment, when the television set speaks, the word is no longer involved, since no dialogue is possible. What we have in these cases is machines that use language as a way of asserting themselves. Their power is magnified, but language is reduced to a useless series of sounds which inspire only reflexes and animal instincts . . .

By its very ambiguity, which is a fundamental and essential part of it, language leaves the listener with a whole margin of freedom. As the speaker, I actually invite my listener to exercise one's liberty in two ways. First, every act of speech supposes either assent or rejection. In other words, of necessity I give my listener a choice to make. A situation where there is choice is a situation where there is freedom. But at the same time, I invite the listener to use the gift of liberty inherent in language, just as I have. The listener must speak in turn, consciously making use of one's freedom. I invite the other to start down the difficult road of self-knowledge and self-expression, of choice, self-exposure, and unveiling.

Language always involves the exercise of freedom. It is never mechanical, just as it is not an object! Subtle structural linguistic analyses are of course limited to texts; that is, to finite, fixed words rather than open-ended ones. Such analyses seem to account for everything: codes, units of meaning, morphemes, etc. But they overlook one thing. Once the languages and lexicons, rhetorics, discourses, and narratives have been stripped of their mystery, one thing is left: language itself. It remains because it is history, and such linguistic analysis excludes history. The word remains because it is a call to freedom, and in such analysis structures and systems are closed. Language is an affirmation of my person, since I am the one speaking, and it is born at the same time as the faint belief, aspiration, or conviction of liberty. The two are born together, and language is a sign bearing witness to my freedom and calling the other person to freedom as well.

This is so true that the word is always paradoxical. This is its second characteristic. The paradox, let us remember, is something situated beside or outside the *doxa* (opinion). The paradox is free of all *doxa*, but at the same time calls the *doxa* into question. Roland Barthes is right in showing that "the real instrument of censorship is the *endoxa* rather than the police." "Just as a language is better defined by what it requires (its obligatory rules) than by what it prohibits (its theoretical rules), in the same way social censorship is present not when one is prevented from speaking, but rather when one is obliged to speak. The deepest subversion (counter-censorship) does not consist so much in saying something to shock opinion, morals, the law, or the police, but in inventing paradoxical speech" . . .

Common sense defies organized thought. Common sense escapes from any sort of integrating doctrine, and, after half a century of oppression, it springs up strangely unharmed and expresses itself in paradoxes. Common sense is not an inferior stage of thought: it is paradox standing up to structured, logical, organized thought, which follows the rules (of logic, dialectic, etc.). Paradox, always related to the word springing up as something new, prevents thought from closing up and reaching completion. Paradox prevents the system from accounting for everything, and does not allow a structure to mold everything.

The poetic word contains paradox within it. You believe poetic language to be insignificant, a side issue in comparison with political and scientific talk? You are right, but poetry continually brings the uncertainty of ambiguity to our attention, along with double meanings, manifold interpretations, false bottoms, and multiple facets. The word is always paradoxical because it corresponds directly to our ambiguity as persons.

Now we are coming to the last characteristic to keep in mind about the word: it is mystery. The most explicit and the best-explained word still brings me inevitably back to mystery. This mystery has to do with the other person, whom I cannot fathom, and whose word provides me with an echo of the other, but only an echo. I perceive this echo, knowing that there is something more. This is the mystery I feel as I recognize spontaneously that I do not understand well or completely what the other person says. There is a mystery for me in my own lack of comprehension, as I become aware of it. How am I going to react? How can I respond? I sense a whole area of mystery in the fact that I am not very sure I understood correctly. I am not very sure about answering. I am not very sure of what I am saying.

There is always a margin around our conversation. More precisely, conversation is like this printed page, framed on all sides by white margins, without words, but which can be filled in with any word at all. The margins situate a conversation and give it the possibility of rebounding and beginning again. They allow the other person to participate with marginal comments. I am aware of this possibility, but I do not know what marginal comments are going to appear beside what I say, changing it. Here again we are dealing with the unexpected. And we come up against the mystery of silence.

The mystery is silence as a break in discourse, not silence in the sense of something that discourse fills up! The enigmatic, disturbing, saddening silence of the other person is an inconvenience as I wait. I expect a response, an explanation, or a statement. The other falls silent, and I no longer know where or how to take my place in relation to the other. More precisely, I no longer know how to *be* as I face the other. I find myself faced with a mystery which eludes me when there is a lull in the conversation. I expect words, but this silence constitutes a chasm in the word, which continues unspoken. It is unheard, but it cannot be eliminated. Thus in all sorts of ways the word is related to mystery. It expresses and engulfs us in mystery.   —*HW*, 23–25

SIGNIFIER AND SIGNIFIED

But we need to go much farther: we have already said that the biblical myths are the signifier of a signified (revealed to faith). We must admit that if God is God, what is revealed does not vary essentially. It is the same yesterday, today, tomorrow.

Then what matters is to know if the existence of what is permanently revealed does not give to the signified a certain power, an orientation, finally a second meaning, which renders it perceptible through the signifier for those who believe what is revealed. In other words, [we must ask] whether what is revealed does not create a much greater possibility of comprehension between contemporary Christians and Christians of the first century than the identity or non-identity of the signifier. At the very most the supposed inadequacy of the signifier would add a supplementary difficulty, but not at all a decisive one. But this position is derived from an inversion of the habitual process. Generally one says: a signifier is transmitted to us that permits us to receive and understand a signified—supposing this path that leads from the signifier to the signified, and an independence of one from the other. Now, I think that the dimension of the Revelation (which I am quite obliged to admit as a Christian!) changes this process: what dominates is the Revealed [One], which posits a certain signified that determines a certain signifier. I therefore have to begin with the Revealed [One] to understand the signifier. It serves nothing to say that it is nevertheless the signifier that enables me to hear the Revealed [One]: no, at the most it is the signified. But in any case I understand nothing of it, whatever be the signifier, if I do not receive and believe the Revealed [One]. And, on the other hand, that implies a union between the signified and the signifier: I cannot choose any one signifier to fit that particular signified. And I cannot then get rid of "metaphysical" myths, concepts from biblical times, as if they were purely cultural, nothing more. I well know that I will be told, "You are talking here about the relationship between the believer today and the believer of the past. But what interests us in the hermeneutical question is the relationship between believer and unbeliever." First of all I believe that this is not entirely exact, for in this genre of research it is always a matter of showing that the biblical texts do not transmit to us the exact contents of revelation for faith. That is always the first step. In the second place, I believe that this is a misapprehension on the part of the hermeneuts: indeed, in this genre of research it is most often a question of the preaching of the message; the intent is to discover (by means of hermeneutics) the message in order to announce it to the nonbelievers in a language that might be accessible to them. Now, this is to expect far too much from hermeneutics. If the message comes from the Revelation of God, hermeneutics can uniquely make the text more clear to me but it can never make it true for me, and it will never make me grasp this message. Therefore, as far as unbelievers are concerned, it permits them only to understand this text logically, rationally, but not at all to receive its message. It will thus not be hermeneutics that will allow the modern unbeliever to have even the least access to the meaning of what is revealed. Now, it is that alone which should matter for a Christian. And it is just this concern that has led many along these paths, but I believe that they are paths that lead nowhere. IF, for faith, the biblical text contains (not in its totality, nor in its plenitude, nor in an obvious way, that goes without saying!) the truth of the Revelation, IF the latter cannot be known by any other way than this text, which itself exists only in accordance with the truth that is Jesus Christ and in referring to him, IF we cannot know Jesus Christ except by means of the Bible, hermeneutics will never deliver to me, as method, the signified of this text, for it is not apt to discern the truth. The decisive point is that by faith *I know* that this Bible *has* a signified, and that the latter *is* truth. Faith *in* Jesus Christ makes me add faith *to* this text. Most certainly there can be misunderstandings concerning interpretation; there can be problems posed about how Jesus Christ is known by this way, but that remains radically secondary, the decisive question being that of the faith which makes me affirm the existence of a true signified. And consequently the path here too, as before, is the inverse of the one that we conceive humanly: instead of saying, "one goes from the signifier to the signified and ultimately from there to the truth," I already said above, "we go from the signified to the signifier." And now we must add, "we go from Jesus Christ the truth to the signified."

—*HQ*, 191–93

6

The New City and Universal Salvation

Toward the end of his life, Jacques Ellul openly shared his belief that Christ's death and resurrection had provided reconciliation for all people—Christians and non-Christians alike. Love, Ellul concluded, was the primary and most foundational characteristic of God's being; and because God is omnipresent and eternal, salvation must be universal. Consequently, Ellul rejected a belief in the existence of a literal hell, instead endorsing the conviction that hell is a state of existence on earth, marked by an ignorance of God's love and of Christ's sacrifice for humanity.

In contrast to his poignant critiques of the present world, Ellul's vision for the future is incredibly hopeful and positive. He describes a forthcoming city where God will bring everything together in harmony: a New Jerusalem where all are united. There we will experience what he calls the calm of the lotus: a state of being absent of tension or struggle, a new reality replete with utter peace.

RECAPITULATION AND THE FUTURE CITY

The doctrine called recapitulation (*anakephalaiosis*) was studied closely by the church fathers. Irenaeus of Lyons especially laid emphasis on this part of Christian teaching. God became man because we could not arrive at immortality and incorruptibility unless he who *is* essentially immortality and incorruptibility joined himself to our nature and to the whole of humanity of which we are a part, and recapitulated it in himself. In the third century Hippolytus insisted on the fact that all humanity (the millions of people that compose it) is resumed, comprehended, and recapitulated in Jesus Christ. The doctrine gradually became weaker and lost its importance, but it has a basis in some passages in Paul. In Christ God accomplished "God's plan for the fullness of time, to unite all things in him, things in heaven and things on earth" (Ephesians 1:10). We have in this verse the Greek equivalent of the word *recapitulate*. Paul is saying that Christ became man, not just to regather all humanity in himself, but to recapitulate all things, all creation, whether things in heaven or things on earth, for human beings do not constitute the whole universe, and it is in this sense that we have to join hands with orthodox theology in calling Christ *Pantocrator*. Christ came not merely to bring human beings to immortality but to bring back the original harmony and unity of things, heeding at last the groaning of a crushed creation. Human beings are saved by Christ, but all that was thrust into disorder and rupture and incoherence is also saved.

This concept of recapitulation corresponds exactly to that of the reconciliation that God effects with creation. "He is before all things, and in him all things hold together. He is the head of the body, the church; he is the beginning, the first-born from the dead, that in everything he might be preeminent. For God willed all fullness [the *pleroma* that corresponds to the totality of creation] to dwell in him, and through him [he willed] to reconcile to himself all things, whether on earth or in heaven, making peace by the blood of his cross" (Colossians 1:17-20). We note the great difference between this cosmic view of reconciliation and that of Irenaeus, which entails only the recapitulation of humanity. Paul says much more. All things subsist in Christ and all things are reconciled in him, both in heaven and on earth. This does not mean that Christ has become as large as creation but that he has become the head of all things, of this great body which is not just the church or humanity, but the whole universe, both material and spiritual. He is the head who directs and impels it, the one from whom thoughts and volitions and decisions emanate. Reconciliation issues in this recapitulation because for once, for the first time, the whole will of God has been fully done with neither break nor hesitation and yet with complete freedom. Jesus was never a serf or a robot. He was never a being that was conditioned to do the will of a God who was a deus ex machina. He did all things with full freedom of decision, choice, love, and truth. He even interpreted freely the commandments that God had given to the Jewish people, and it was thus that he was fully obedient. He was the perfect image of God. For the first time since the fall of Adam God found his image again, his counterpart, his free and creative partner in prayer and decision. In this shattered universe it was enough that for once the will of God was fully done. Order was then restored, reconciliation was made, and recapitulation could take place . . .

At the same time, the position of theologians like Irenaeus has to be regarded as one of realism, not in the modern sense, but in that of the debate between nominalism and realism. On this view, humanity is a reality, a real entity and not an intellectual abstraction. On the one side there are individual people and on the other a coherent whole which has its own existence, which is different from the sum of individuals, which has its own qualities and specificity, which is a "rational being" and "moral person," and it is this entity, already unified and real, that is assumed in recapitulation. At different times I myself have already declared in favor of nominalism. One can talk about humanity, but in itself it is merely a word, which is useful for the purpose of denoting the totality of people, and which serves well in reflection and communication, but which is never anything more. The millions of individuals do not constitute one real humanity. Nor is there one human nature that is always identical and immutable and that one can find in each individual. Nor is there any rational being that is the same through space and time. For me, such things are mere names and no more . . .

In my view this seems to be shown by the following conviction. God loves us. God loves us fully. And when I say that, I am saying that God does not love a kind of phantom, an evanescent and abstract being with a common nature. Loving us, God loves us in the concreteness of our lives, with all that makes up our lives, our jobs, our hobbies, our hopes, our fears, the things we have created, the beings we have loved. God loves us in the totality of our lives. Thus God does not save an abstract and interchangeable phantom. God loves us in our individuality, that is, in our history *with* its works. Saved people are not judged to be of value apart from their works. The judgment would be terrible if God did not think that any of our works deserved to be saved, conserved. A whole life lived in vain! The result of so many hours and so much energy reduced to nothing! . . .

God has granted us independence to lead our own lives, to undertake our own works, to build up our own histories. This is a false independence in view of the many determinations imposed by the orders to which we are subject, yet God still grants it, and the more so if we turn to God, for then we receive not merely independence but freedom. In this case we do works that are our own, that God neither expects nor dictates, but that God does not necessarily judge to be bad because they are independent. As speaking beings we have been called upon to cooperate with God from the very beginning of creation (for this is the point of Adam's naming of the animals in Genesis). Even after the fall we have still been called upon to cooperate with God (we are God's co-workers, says Paul in 1 Corinthians 3:9). God issues directives, gives signs, makes appeals, and sometimes intervenes, for God always expects us to do God's work. We finally cooperate with God in erecting this perfect Jerusalem, for if it is exclusively God's work, God builds it with the materials that we bring, materials of all kinds which, when approved by God, reveal a certain human greatness which is our glory . . .

In other words, at the end of time God will place us not in a garden but in a city. God has changed the plan. Why? Because in this new creation, God takes human history and human works into account. One might say with some truth that the city is the chief human work. It was with the appearance of the city that the true history of human development began. The city is the focus of all invention and interchange and art; the city is the birthplace of culture. I am not saying that there is no rural culture, but it arises in symbiosis with urban culture. The city is indeed our primary human creation. It is a uniquely human world. It is the symbol that we have chosen, the place that we have invented and that we prefer.   —*WIB*, 214–15, 216–27, 219, 223

THE NEW JERUSALEM

Throughout Scripture (and here again I refer to what I have shown elsewhere) the city is the instrument of the revolt of humans against God. On the one hand, it is the world of humans, which humans have desired to set up as a counter-creation with the distinct will to exclude God; on the other hand, it is the point of crystallization of the pride and power of human beings. The city is the negation of the omnipotence of God; it is the closed door of humankind's walling itself up against any relation with the Creator. Biblically, it is the place of the curse, pitiless, the place of war and oppression, of wealth and slavery. And the judgment responds to that; Babylon is judged as incarnation of the powers; it is also a city. Such is the decision of God. And this double image: judgment of the city Babylon—re-creation of the city Jerusalem shows at what point the symbol of the city is central here. This new creation signifies, then, that God *reverses* what had been the instrument of revolt in order to make of it the work of reconciliation. Such is the meaning of the judgment. It is not an abolition, and then God makes something else. No! It is a destruction of meaning and a re-creation of meaning. That which was the obstinate image of the negation of humankind against God is denied in itself and becomes the opening of the identity "God with us." Humans had desired to make a work of evil and revolt, of rupture with God. But God makes this project end in its opposite. But not by the manifestation of God's greater power: there is here no competition of powers. God does not seek in the apocalyptic events to prove that God is the stronger one. That would be absurd, mediocre, and perfectly inadequate for the God of Jesus Christ! But God invests this work of humans with God's love. For what greater attestation of love than to take from the enemy the weapon of war in order to make of it the very means of absolute, limitless reconciliation! God gives to the city the potential of love. But in doing this God carries the work of humankind to its perfection. Jerusalem is the perfect city as no human city has ever been able to be. But in addition it answers that which had been the fundamental intention of humans. Because if, from one side, humans in building the city made of it a work against God, from the other, humans had intended to make of it the place of their perfect communication, their communion, their assembly; finally, this is exactly what God does with the heavenly Jerusalem. Humans had never succeeded; humans had always experienced failure, and the actual urban monstrosity is striking testimony to this. Thus that which had been the historical failure of humans becomes the triumphant success; there is finally communion, there is finally assembly (and not only of one generation, but of all). Thus God grants in the heavenly Jerusalem that which had been the purpose of humans, that which had been the human's patient search through all civilizations, that which had been both hope and expectation. God does not fabricate an abstract place, outside of any relation with humans: God is not paternalistic. God answers the intention that humans had in building Babel: "to make a name," and God gives humans a new name. To create the place of human community, God creates total communion. The city was a place of the dissolution of specificities, of the meeting and mixture of all ideas, values, races, social categories: it receives its complete fulfillment. For in this New Jerusalem all races, peoples, nations, tribes meet. But while the tendency was always toward unity by the disappearance of diversities, now unity appears (in God) in the communion of existing diversities, and human plurality is maintained. We have already encountered several times this relation of the harmony of the one and the many in John's Apocalypse. The New Jerusalem resembles Babylon. Without the corruption of Babylon. Without the will to Power. And this new city then represents the totality of Meaning.

—*ABR*, 223–24

UNIVERSAL SALVATION

I am taking up here a basic theme that I have dealt with elsewhere but which is so essential that I have no hesitation in repeating myself. It is the recognition that all people from the beginning of time are saved by God in Jesus Christ, that they have all been recipients of his grace no matter what they have done. This is a scandalous proposition. It shocks our spontaneous sense of justice. The guilty ought to be punished. How can Hitler and Stalin be among the saved? The just ought to be recognized as such and the wicked condemned. But in my view this is purely human logic which simply shows that there is no understanding of salvation by grace or of the meaning of the death of Jesus Christ . . .

If God is God, the Almighty, the Creator of all things, the Omnipresent, then we can think of no place or being whatever outside God. If there were a place outside, God would not be all in all, the Creator of all things. How can we think of God creating a place or being where God is not present? What, then, about hell? Either it is in God, in which case God is not universally good, or it is outside God, hell having often been defined as the place where God is not. But the latter is completely unthinkable . . .

God is love. This is the central revelation. How can we conceive of God who is love ceasing to love one of God's creatures? How can we think that God can cease to love the creation that God has made in his own image? This would be a contradiction in terms. God cannot cease to be love. . . . Nothing can exist outside God's love, for God is all in all. It is unthinkable that there should exist a place of suffering, of torment, of the domination of evil, of beings that merely hate since their only function is to torture. It is astounding that Christian theology should not have seen at a glance how impossible this idea is. Being love, God cannot send to hell the creation which God so loved that God gave his only Son for it. God cannot reject it because it is God's creation . . .

It is certain that being saved or lost does not depend on our own free decision. I believe that all people are included in the grace of God. I believe that all the theologies that have made a large place for damnation and hell are unfaithful to a theology of grace. For if there is predestination to perdition, there is no salvation by grace. Salvation by grace is granted precisely to those who without grace would have been lost. Jesus did not come to seek the righteous and the saints, but sinners. He came to seek those who in strict justice ought to have been condemned. A theology of grace implies universal salvation. What could grace mean if it were granted only to some sinners and not to others according to an arbitrary decree that is totally contrary to the nature of our God? If grace is granted according to the greater or lesser number of sins, it is no longer grace—it is just the opposite because of this accountancy. Paul is the very one who reminds us that the enormity of the sin is no obstacle to grace: "Where sin increased, grace abounded all the more" (Romans 5:20). This is the key statement. The greater the sin, the more God's love reveals itself to be far beyond any judgment or evaluation of ours. This grace covers all things. It is thus effectively universal. I do not think that in regard to this grace we can make the Scholastic distinctions between prevenient grace, expectant grace, conditional grace, etc. Such adjectives weaken the thrust of the free grace of the absolute sovereign, and they result only from our great difficulty in believing that God has done everything. But this means that nothing in God's creation is excluded or lost . . .

Those who believe live in hope. They have already the first fruits of eternal life. They have within them that which will not perish, the Word of God. They live a double life on earth; in this world which is saved in the eyes of some and is terrifying in the eyes of the rest; on the earth on which some have assurance of the resurrection and the rest only the certainty of death; on the earth on which some see meaning in the human venture because they have the light, and the rest wander in folly and "perdition" because they cannot see the way. But this is a temporary situation in human life. All are encompassed in "God so loved the world and Jesus came to save the world." In the course of human history there are those who are lost on a way with no exit. But the latter are not lost to the heart of God, nor are they outside the love of God. As has often been said, what we suffer here on earth is punishment enough. Hell is on earth, as the Bible itself tells us . . .

Although I proclaim the truth of universal salvation, I cannot proclaim it as an absolute truth. I cannot penetrate the secret of God. I cannot presume upon a simple decision of the eternal God. Hence I cannot proclaim this truth as a dogmatic proposition which is scientifically demonstrated. In proclaiming it, I am saying what I believe, what meditation on the biblical texts leads me to believe. I do not teach universal salvation; I announce it.

—WIB, 188, 189, 190, 193, 207

THE DESIRE FOR ETERNITY

Concepts like the absolute, the infinite, and "eternity" can of course be represented mathematically, but Jewish thought, and the Christian thought that follows it, are *historical*. Entrance into the heavenly Jerusalem does nothing to change that. The history of "God with humanity" continues, but in another vein. Thus the desire God places in our heart does not focus on stopping time, but on a life of indefinite, unlimited duration, on *total time,* which truly has no end—no conceivable end, and no certain end. Our desire for eternity has to do with ourselves, those we love, and our work—living things. This desire amounts to the will to live, contradicting the idea that there is a time for each thing, but that this time is soon over (and that the time for the opposite activity will soon end as well).

The desire for eternity is not limited to Judeo–Christian thought. We need to realize that people belonging to a wide variety of societies and cultures experience it. When Hitler spoke of the Millennium of the Reich, he expressed this desire. So did Marx when he declared that humanity had been living in prehistory and that human history would begin with the founding of communism. In communist society there would be no more dialectical mutation, yet history would not be abolished. We sense the same desire for eternity in the Vietcong's marching song, "May Uncle Ho live ten thousand years," and in the Egyptian practice of embalming bodies so they could take a trip that would last indefinitely. They all desired endless duration rather than some metaphysical eternity. They wanted to vanquish time so it would no longer be their master . . .

Our desire for eternity remains only that. This time with no beginning and no end, this indefinite duration we desire, remains out of reach, so we feel tortured, like Tantalus . . . On its own, our desire cannot be attained. Realizing this limitation is part of wisdom, as we know. But now we take a further step: realizing this means arriving at certainty concerning God. This contradiction, between what exists and what we long and hope for, testifies that God is there in our silence, absence, and ignorance.

So we do not wait for some nondescript, meaningless eternity that would have value in itself. Our desire does not express our paranoia, or a return to our origins (which are hidden!). Rather, it is the secret call God has placed in our heart. A call to something utterly "other," which we cannot define, grasp, or invent. Thus at the bottom of wisdom, as it bears pitiless witness to reality, we find a way of access to this other world.

If we have to give a name to what results from the rigors of wisdom, we might call it an existential theology. It is not a negative theology—stating that we know nothing of God holds no interest for us. But stating that we have an emptiness within us, a torn or broken place, and that we *are not* mere rotating physiological organisms or collections of neurons—this understanding leads us deep into truth. Nothomb forcefully reminds us that "every desire amounts to a lack, and every lack implies a presence somewhere. A lack corresponds to a fullness rather than an emptiness."

We must not neglect another aspect of the Hebrew word translated "eternity" *('olam):* specialists all connect it with the root *'lm,* meaning "to hide," which we will consider later. Eternity, then, represents what is hidden from us: what we are ignorant of. Not just a hidden time or a hidden work, but *what* is hidden, as opposed to everything conceivable and visible, related to our hands and our works.

Consequently, even if we could convince ourselves that we rule over time through mathematics, for example, or that we know the sum total of human history, down to its smallest details, we still would have failed to grasp eternity. Eternity would still elude us because it remains as hidden as the God who put it in our heart and who leads us down the path of wisdom.

—RB, 245–47

THE CALM OF THE LOTUS

"Negativism! Again this time, everything you have said is negative: iconoclasm, struggling against the closing up of language, fighting the irrationality of the lunatic's language, and what else? What positive proposals do you have, and what program do you suggest?" I could answer in learned fashion with the positivistic dialectic of negativism: in the final analysis, only the No produces change and advance.

Again in this case, however, I prefer to refer to the simplest of images: a person is chained fast, by his feet and wrists, with forged chains. He has no way of freeing himself. You come with a sledgehammer and you break his chains. At the material level your act is purely and exclusively negative: you have broken some chains that were a fine product of human technique. You have destroyed the work of an artisan or of a large business concern that shows human progress. You are entirely negative—especially since you do nothing else. You have broken a lovely iron object that is now useless. And there you stopped. You have constructed nothing positive, that's certain.

But was I also supposed to take the freed prisoner by the hand, make him my pupil, and teach him what he should and could do? Doesn't this purely negative deed produce freedom? Now that he is unfettered, the person can stand up, begin to walk, and choose where he wants to go; he could do none of this before. Well, let him do it! But only *he* can do it, and if he prefers to stay hunched up in his prison wishing for his chains back, what further positive deed can I do for him?

This is precisely our situation. Whoever accuses my analyses and research of negativism and considers iconoclasm and the criticism of structuralist ideologies or of romanticizing insanity to be a purely pessimistic orientation proves just one thing: that he loves his chains. That person is not ready to risk the adventure of freedom that begins with the freedom of the word, which requires a great effort and an enormous commitment!

The only positive action we can take is to open a space into which we must dash forward. In this manner we can discover the word's real nature, the unparalleled risk of truth and falsehood, and the extraordinary adventure of rationalizing or freeing from slavery. This is the open space before us. It requires a dialectical advance of our minds that are accustomed to the linear technological process; it requires the reintegration of the temporal into a spatially oriented civilization; and it forbids us to stop in our tracks.

As soon as the word becomes free again, we are involved in a whole set of contradictions. But they are necessary for life, particularly for life in the midst of division, such as the division caused by the smashing of the monolithic audiovisual world. Since the word is made to unfold and develop endlessly, we must continually refuse to stop. A spatial orientation presupposes stopping in the place which finally suits us. The visual world involves stopping; I must freeze and frame things. But the word stops no more than time does. No instant can last, nor can time be suspended. The word is the same. We must move ahead to meet what is advancing toward us: the great eschatological recapitulation of human history.

Today we live in division and contradiction the life that one day will be unity, balance, and peace. We live in tension the life that promises a flowering . . . We live in dialectic what will be the calm of the lotus flower. We live in conflict the life that promises reconciliation. We must not refuse this single possible mode of living: division, tension, and dialectic, as they are expressed and implied by the word. For apart from this mode all that exists is petrification, rigidity, decomposition, and death.

We can live this life only to the degree that we know that the reconciliation is already won, and that in Jesus Christ word and sight, proclamation and experience, space and time, are united. We need to know that we will see this reconciliation, that we "will understand fully, even as [we] have been fully understood," that we will see "face to face" what we have heard about (1 Corinthians 13:12). Job says: "I had heard of you by the hearing of the ear, but now my eyes see you" (Job 42:5). Based on this certainty, without which we have nothing to live for and without which the conflict would be intolerable, we can return to the daily struggle to make the word resound, alone and unshackled. During the space of time that separates us from this final sight, may the word resound for human freedom and for God's truth.

—*HW*, 268–69

MODERN SPIRITUAL MASTERS
Robert Ellsberg, Series Editor

This series introduces the essential writing and vision of some of the great spiritual teachers of our time. While many of these figures are rooted in long-established traditions of spirituality, others have charted new, untested paths. In each case, however, they have engaged in a spiritual journey shaped by the challenges and concerns of our age. Together with the saints and witnesses of previous centuries, these modern spiritual masters may serve as guides and companions to a new generation of seekers.

Already published:
Modern Spiritual Masters (edited by Robert Ellsberg)
Swami Abhishiktananda (edited by Shirley du Boulay)
Metropolitan Anthony of Sourozh (edited by Gillian Crow)
Eberhard Arnold (edited by Johann Christoph Arnold)
Pedro Arrupe (edited by Kevin F. Burke, S.J.)
Daniel Berrigan (edited by John Dear)
Thomas Berry (edited by Mary EvelynTucker and John Grim)
Dietrich Bonhoeffer (edited by Robert Coles)
Robert McAfee Brown (edited by Paul Crowley)
Dom Helder Camara (edited by Francis McDonagh)
Carlo Carretto (edited by Robert Ellsberg)
G. K. Chesterton (edited by William Griffin)
Joan Chittister (edited by Mary Lou Kownacki and Mary
    Hembrow Snyder)
Yves Congar (edited by Paul Lakeland)
The Dalai Lama (edited by Thomas A. Forsthoefel)
Alfred Delp, S.J. (introduction by Thomas Merton)
Catherine de Hueck Dogerty (edited by David Meconi, S.J.)
Virgilio Elizondo (edited by Timothy Matovina)
Jacques Ellul (edited by Jacob E. Van Vleet)
Ralph Waldo Emerson (edited by Jon M. Sweeney)
Charles de Foucauld (edited by Robert Ellsberg)
Mohandas Gandhi (edited by John Dear)
Bede Griffiths (edited by Thomas Matus)
Romano Guardini (edited by Robert A. Krieg)
Gustavo Gutiérrez (edited by Daniel G. Groody)

Thich Nhat Hanh (edited by Robert Ellsberg)
Abraham Joshua Heschel (edited by Susannah Heschel)
Etty Hillesum (edited by Annemarie S. Kidder)
Caryll Houselander (edited by Wendy M. Wright)
Pope John XXIII (edited by Jean Maalouf)
Rufus Jones (edited by Kerry Walters)
Clarence Jordan (edited by Joyce Hollyday)
John Main (edited by Laurence Freeman)
Anthony de Mello (edited by William Dych, S.J.)
Thomas Merton (edited by Christine M. Bochen)
John Muir (edited by Tim Flinders)
John Henry Newman (edited by John T. Ford, C.S.C.)
Henri Nouwen (edited by Robert A. Jonas)
Flannery O'Connor (edited by Robert Ellsberg)
Karl Rahner (edited by Philip Endean)
Brother Roger of Taizé (edited by Marcello Fidanzio)
Oscar Romero (by Marie Dennis, Rennie Golden, and Scott
    Wright)
Albert Schweitzer (edited by James Brabazon)
Frank Sheed and Maisie Ward (edited by David Meconi)
Sadhu Sundar Singh (edited by Charles E. Moore)
Mother Maria Skobtsova (introduction by Jim Forest)
Dorothee Soelle (edited by Dianne L. Oliver)
Edith Stein (edited by John Sullivan, O.C.D.)
David Steindl-Rast (edited by Clare Hallward)
William Stringfellow (edited by Bill Wylie-Kellerman)
Pierre Teilhard de Chardin (edited by Ursula King)
Mother Teresa (edited by Jean Maalouf)
St. Thérèse of Lisieux (edited by Mary Frohlich)
Phyllis Tickle (edited by Jon M. Sweeney)
Henry David Thoreau (edited by Tim Flinders)
Howard Thurman (edited by Mary Krohlich)
Leo Tolstoy (edited by Charles E. Moore)
Evelyn Underhill (edited by Emilie Griffin)
Vincent Van Gogh (by Carol Berry)
Jean Vanier (edited by Carolyn Whitney-Brown)
Swami Vivekananda (edited by Victor M. Parachin)
Simone Weil (edited by Eric O. Springsted)
John Howard Yoder (edited by Paul Martens and Jenny Howells)